Advance Praise for *Understanding Your Attachment Style*

"Marc Cameron has a way of making complex theories understandable and actionable. He has done that for attachment styles in a way that helps people understand their relational struggles and apply the solutions for improvement. I highly recommend this book for anyone who wants more harmony in their homes."

—Dr. Alice Benton, PsyD, author of *Understanding and Loving Your Child in a Screen-Saturated World*

"*Understanding Your Attachment Style* is a masterful blend of clinical expertise, practical tools, and heartfelt wisdom. Marc Cameron has created an invaluable guide for anyone seeking to understand their attachment patterns and build healthier, more secure relationships.

"As a trauma-informed, attachment-based therapist, I deeply appreciate the way Marc integrates decades of research with compassionate, real-world application. He provides not just insight, but a clear, actionable path toward healing and growth—whether you're navigating intimate relationships, family dynamics, parenting, or your own personal journey.

"Marc's authenticity and lived experience make this book uniquely powerful. He writes with both the authority of a seasoned clinician and the empathy of someone who has done the work himself. This is a must-read for anyone who desires deeper self-awareness, healthier connections, and the freedom that comes from secure attachment."

—Dr. Jacqui Mack-Harris, PsyD, Licensed Marriage and Family Therapist, Clinical Supervisor, and Educator

Understanding Your Attachment Style

Understanding Your Attachment Style

The Path to Overcoming Unhelpful Patterns and Building Healthy, Secure Relationships

Marc Cameron

Nashville   New York

> While all the case studies shared in this book are based on real interactions, names and details have been changed, and in some cases patient stories have been combined and/or conflated.

Copyright © 2025 by Marc Cameron

Jacket copyright © 2025 by Hachette Book Group, Inc.
Jacket design by Whitney J. Hicks. Jacket artwork by Shutterstock.

Hachette Book Group supports the right to free expression and the value of copyright. The purpose of copyright is to encourage writers and artists to produce the creative works that enrich our culture.

The scanning, uploading, and distribution of this book without permission is a theft of the author's intellectual property. If you would like permission to use material from the book (other than for review purposes), please contact permissions@hbgusa.com. Thank you for your support of the author's rights.

Worthy Books
Hachette Book Group
1290 Avenue of the Americas
New York, NY 10104
worthypublishing.com
X.com/WorthyPub

First Edition: December 2025

Worthy Books is a division of Hachette Book Group, Inc. The Worthy Books name and logo are trademarks of Hachette Book Group, Inc.

The publisher is not responsible for websites (or their content) that are not owned by the publisher.

The Hachette Speakers Bureau provides a wide range of authors for speaking events. To find out more, go to hachettespeakersbureau.com or email HachetteSpeakers@hbgusa.com.

Print book interior designed by Bart Dawson

Library of Congress Control Number: 2025944871

ISBN: 9781546008569 (Hardcover)
ISBN: 9781546008583 (E-Book)
ISBN: 9781668652558 (Downloadable Audio)

Printed in the United States of America

LSC-C

Printing 1, 2025

To Milan and Kay for introducing me to attachment in a way that opened my eyes so vividly, and to my family, Amy, Kaytlin, and Carter, for unwittingly providing me the opportunities to practice growing from my insecure attachment.

Contents

Foreword • xiii

Introduction • xvii

Step One
Develop Insight

Chapter One: How We Attach (or Don't) • 3

Chapter Two: The Cycle of Bonding • 19

Chapter Three: Reprogramming the Amygdala • 33

Chapter Four: Knowing Thyself • 45

Step Two
Become More Aware

Chapter Five: Avoiders Feel "Fine" • 63

Chapter Six: Pleasers Want to Help You Feel Better • 81

Chapter Seven: Vacillators Long for More • 99

Chapter Eight: Controllers and Victims Facing Their Unsolvable Struggle (Disorganized Attachment) • 119

Chapter Nine: Security Is Still Possible—The Secure Connector • 137

Step Three
Show Up to Practice

Chapter Ten: Growth Goals • 155

Chapter Eleven: Resistance • 177

Chapter Twelve: Rewiring Neural Pathways • 193

Chapter Thirteen: The Importance of Repair • 205

Chapter Fourteen: Measuring Progress and Avoiding Pitfalls • 217

Appendix: Needs for Emotions Chart • 237
Appendix: The Cycle of How We Try to Get Our Needs Met • 239
Appendix: Attachment Assessment • 241
About the Author • 243

Understanding Your Attachment Style

Foreword

Years ago, as director of our counseling center, Relationship 180, I received a call from Marc Cameron informing me his men's group was reading our book, *How We Love*. Bursting with enthusiasm he told me that for the first time in his life he finally understood himself and the root of the frustrating dynamic in his marriage. He went on to say one of the descriptions in our book explained his early experiences and his reactivity in adult life that sabotaged relationships. In addition to a successful career in corporate America, he had also completed a degree in counseling and was working to complete his three thousand post graduate hours. He then asked me for a position as an associate at Relationship 180. I told him I was honored to receive his call, but we needed someone with more clinical experience. I invited him to call me back in a year and wondered if he'd follow up.

Then came the call: "Hello Milan, this is Marc Cameron, you told me to call you back in a year." After multiple interviews, we hired Marc, who worked under one of our supervisors until he was fully licensed as a Marriage and Family Therapist. In time, we met his lovely wife, Amy, and we could see they had become close as a couple having worked through the steps in *How We Love* to create a *securely bonded* friendship and marriage. Let me be clear here, there are therapists and authors who have a formal education and are licensed to practice, and there are those who have been educated, licensed, and who have *applied attachment research in their lives*, to better their marriage and parenting. Marc and Amy are in the second group.

Marc is an avid reader who stays current with relational research and has a successful practice where people are truly helped. With a full client load and many referrals from satisfied clients, he is most qualified to author this book. Having experienced a change in himself and in his marriage, he is enthusiastic about sharing this transformational journey with you. As a co-host on New Life Live radio, he is also able to share his wisdom with callers like you who feel pain and need hope.

Understanding Your Attachment Style begins with *Insight*, where you will learn how early relational imprints are formed, why attunement to yours and other's emotions is a key to healthiness, how bonding takes place, how our brain's wiring system can hijack good intentions, and the emotional intelligence needed to overcome these unhelpful traits.

Attachment research has been taking place in universities worldwide for eighty years. In the *Awareness* section, Marc will explain the attachment styles common to us all but that fail to serve us well as adults. You will be amazed as you read the descriptions, and you will find relief knowing there are millions just like you. Not because misery loves company, but with a diagnosis, there is a cure.

Finally, there is HOPE as Marc reveals solutions for relational success, and the new *Practices* we all need to employ to grow out of our early imprints. You will learn growth goals, how new brain pathways are formed, what true repair can do for a relationship, and how to measure progress along the way.

Marc's wife, Amy Cameron, is a Psychiatric Mental Health Nurse Practitioner, who sees patients, provides counsel, and is licensed to prescribe medications. Together they make a powerful duo, and we are so impressed with them, as we move into retirement, we are passing them the baton of ownership and stewardship of the How We Love brand, website, and products provided at www.howwelove.com.

There is a bike store owner in our town whose TV commercials feature him in a wild outfit, jumping up and down and yelling, "Buy my bikes, buy my bikes!" Now imagine me, jumping up and down in front of my computer yelling, "Buy this book, buy this book!" You won't regret it.

Milan & Kay Yerkovich
Recovering Pleaser and Recovering Avoider
March 12, 2025

Introduction

Each year, for about fifteen years, I made a promise to myself that this would be the year I conquered my reactivity. I knew I disliked some of the ways I behaved at times, and getting married and having kids only seemed to bring out more of this unwanted behavior in me. Trying harder to "love" better didn't seem to help, because I couldn't do what I hadn't yet learned.

Then I read *How We Love* by Milan and Kay Yerkovich. I was stunned. The Vacillator chapter described me in ways I'd never been able to articulate yet instantly recognized as true. It also exposed the predictable conflict pattern that my wife, Amy, and I were stuck in and outlined a process we could begin using together to work through it. However, it quickly became clear we both struggled with some basic, well-known healthy communication practices. I realized that for me to effectively engage in the healing and reconditioning process, I needed to learn how to show up more securely in *all* my relationships. This meant I had to do my own internal work. After all, how could I help others as a therapist if I hadn't been on the path of growth myself? That realization set me on a deeper mission to understand the growth process for an individual.

For those who are unmarried, are getting married, have an unwilling spouse, or are simply looking to apply this material more widely, I hope this can be the resource to help guide your growth, encourage those around you into secure attachment, and even help you pick healthier connections.

To begin with the initial question that started it all, what if I were to tell you the struggles in your relationships may have less to do with your *willingness* to work things out, and more to do with how your reactions were *programmed* as a child? If that were true, you might be unknowingly playing out a similar pattern with people for years without knowing why or what to do to improve things. In fact, if you're like many people I encounter in therapy, you might have only poor modeling to draw from, with few or no memories of being comforted after experiencing hurt or distress in your early life, or with experiences of being abandoned or rebuffed.

Those who do have many memories of comfort likely had parents who were attuned to them growing up, which has given them a solid foundation of positive experiences to tap into in adulthood to calm themselves when they get stressed. These individuals have learned to securely attach to others in how they express their emotions and request their needs. If you did not have many experiences of comfort and soothing after stressful events, or inconsistency from a parent, research shows that you'll have a **learned insecurity** in your attachment style that affects your relationships with self and others. And this isn't your fault.

See if you relate to any of these common struggles.

Heather's family bails on the delicious dinner she'd prepared. She feels deeply disappointed. These disappointments happen a lot for Heather in all areas of her life. She wonders why she keeps setting herself up for letdowns and why things can't just turn out the way she pictures at least some of the time.

Brian comes home from work and keeps his complaints to himself. But his wife, Stacy, wants more from him and says he doesn't "emotionally connect" with her. He's not sure what this means. He reasons he is a good provider and low-maintenance with needs. He works forty-five hours a week and takes his turn to run the kids around to their activities; however, it feels like Stacy constantly wants more from him.

Karen is experienced in her job and newly promoted as manager of her department. She tries to keep everyone in her team happy, but inevitably someone seems dissatisfied. Because she feels anxious when others are upset at her, she tries to juggle everyone's desires, but it results in her own detriment. She stays stuck giving and giving, feeling like it's never enough to please others.

So many people are stuck in cycles they feel powerless to change. They don't realize their expectations have been shaped by their upbringings, so they feel like others are mis-attuned to them. Attunement is the feeling when another person understands what you need and provides it. If only they could get in sync with others they might feel that somebody finally "got" them. And this is why most people arrive in my office for therapy, often without even being able to articulate the real problem.

> So many people are stuck in cycles they feel powerless to change.

If you feel the people in your life are *attuned* to you, you will feel strongly attached to them. If you don't, you won't. In this book, I want to show you how our childhood experiences with primary caregivers continue to affect our relationships with others in adulthood. The attachment programming that was involuntarily imprinted on you shapes your adult behaviors in ways that hinder and damage the connections you need to feel known and secure. But the great news is you don't have to remain stuck!

Now, some people might be skeptical and wonder, "How can my childhood, which happened so long ago, still be affecting my relationships today?" That's a fair question, and it deserves a thoughtful, thorough answer. In fact, it's such an important question that we'll spend the next few chapters unpacking it together. So hang with me, it's worth the journey. But let's say you are willing to acknowledge that you have an insecure attachment style—how then do you move toward developing a secure attachment? Decades of attachment research shows that you *earn* secure attachment through building a *coherent narrative of your childhood experiences.* Let's break this phrase down. "Coherent" means something makes sense. And a "narrative" is a story. So, by *making sense of your childhood story*, you lay the foundation to earn a secure attachment. Neurobiology studies reinforce the attachment research and show change is possible because our brains remain neuroplastic for our entire lives, meaning they are continually shaped as we learn. So, even if you developed an insecure attachment style, you have the power to grow and *earn* secure attachment through understanding, self-awareness, and practical steps. My hope is this book will equip you with the knowledge and tools to do that so you can finally break free from old patterns, build healthier relationships, and experience deeper emotional connection.

What does it mean to "earn" secure attachment? Think for a moment about the accomplishment you are most proud of. Part of your pride, I'm sure, has to do with the amount of effort and dedication you applied to achieving it. Unlike a gift you are given, it's a reward you *earned* through your own hard work. Too many people approach relationships with a "gift" mindset, believing relationship success is determined by fate (the universe's or God's introduction) or luck (a chance meeting with the "right person" at the "right time"). Website algorithms may provide better odds of someone you think is compatible for you, but this is still more of a lottery approach than a skill.

If you believe relationships depend on compatibility, luck, or fate, you need to know that *finding* a good relationship is not as dependable as creating one. While attraction, similar interests, and shared life goals absolutely help, the real key to good relationships lies in learning what it means to securely attach.

The *Oxford Dictionary* defines *compatibility* as "a state in which two things are able to exist or occur together **without problems or conflict**." Many people interpret this to mean similarities two people share rather than the ability to understand, navigate, and accept differences. When people are truly compatible, they've developed skills to compromise, problem-solve, take turns, share, respect each other's boundaries, take responsibility, offer forgiveness, and make strong commitments to grow personally even when feeling let down by the other or having opposing perspectives—these are the qualities of secure attachment.

People who approach relationships this way truly understand compatibility. They understand that an emotionally secure relationship can only form between two emotionally secure individuals, because when one or both partners are emotionally insecure, the relationship is inevitably built on an insecure foundation. Emotionally secure people see relational red flags earlier and avoid spending much time pursuing relationships not likely to last, because they know the math simply doesn't work any other way.

If you'll take the time to examine your relationships and see what attachment style tendencies you've developed—whether that's emotional avoidance, people-pleasing, relational-idealism that causes you to vacillate between what you want, or being an authoritarian controller or helpless victim—you can change. **Recognize you can only intentionally change something you are aware of.** And when you uncover how your attachments in childhood created *learned emotional insecurity*, you will see how *earned security* is developed, and how to overcome the patterns that are keeping you stuck. By understanding how the stability of your connections to your caregivers formed from their responses (or lack thereof) to your needs, you will discover the path to security in adult relationships. Even though most parents tried their best, if we were not nurtured into the security we needed as children, we carry impaired patterns of relating into adulthood.

Before we move on, let's define a few key terms I'll use throughout this book:

> *Self-protective strategies* are actions we take to keep ourselves emotionally safe when facing emotional discomfort or perceived relational threat.

Reactivity refers to these strategies having become automatic over time from repeated use.

While, *responding* is assessing a situation free of these automatic adaptations.

We all have developed some automatic behaviors to protect ourselves from the pain caused by early relational wounds. Ironically, it's these same learned self-protective strategies that were once adaptive which often prevent our adult relationships from feeling safe, reciprocal, and emotionally fulfilling at times. The key to growth is learning to recognize these and respond instead, which allows you to recondition old patterns and move toward greater emotionally security.

This book's three sections—*Develop Insight, Become More Aware,* and *Show Up to Practice*—are steps that, when applied, will help define how you can create secure attachments in all your relationships. If you know how to drive, think about how you first learned. Imagine if no one told you how the car operated, the rules of the road, or what was required to drive safely to get where you were going. You'd have to pick it up all on your own. First and foremost, you'd need some **insight**—foundational knowledge into how the car worked. Then you'd need to become **aware of yourself and others in this environment**—how roads operate, how well you drive, and how other drivers behave and respond to your driving.

Still, even with insight, self-awareness, *and* other-awareness, we need many months of showing up to **practice** before we're comfortable enough with this new skill to manage independently. Practice is the only way to turn knowledge and awareness into a new, confident automatic behavior. Once you understand what makes relationships work, and become aware of patterns and ways to improve them, you can begin to take action to grow. And my promise to you is that if you will read and implement these three steps, you will grow! Here's the magic formula:

Insight + Awareness + Practice = Growth

In Step One, *Develop Insight*, I'll explain how attachment programming works, so you can recognize how your ability to relate and securely attach was impacted by your past bonding experiences, and understand why you feel and act the way you do. When Heather gained insight that repeatedly being let down by her father in childhood had created a disappointment trigger in her, she felt relief knowing there was a reason for feeling such strong emotion over minor events.

In Step Two, *Become More Aware*, we'll cover the attachment styles, how each is formed, and how they affect relationships. As Brian began to understand that healthy relationships require strong emotional connections for intimacy, he became aware he was being dismissive of Stacy's emotions, focusing on acts of service rather than getting to know her deeply on an emotional level.

Then in Step Three, *Show Up to Practice*, we'll look at the reconditioning work that leads to growth, and how to break our automatic thinking and reactivity. When Karen learned to say no confidently to people's requests in order to manage her own needs, and accept their disappointment wasn't something she was responsible to fix, she was finally able to balance the needs of her department, and her anxiety reduced.

By learning some new powerful strategies, you can make the shift from reacting to responding and feeling secure inside, even when not entirely in control of all outcomes. It will feel challenging at first, but those who stick with it will discover a freedom from patterns that have bound them for years.

In the Appendix, you'll find an attachment assessment, and at the end of each chapter, I'll also offer some reflection questions that you can explore in a separate journal or if reading with a group. These are designed to help you understand how your past is impacting your present, so you can develop your coherent narrative.

Even though you didn't choose to develop an insecure attachment, you can choose to grow toward security. Please understand, there's no promise that others will do their part just because you do yours. Growth happens when you choose to do this work for yourself, no matter what anyone else does. Only once we become more dissatisfied with our own reactive patterns than we are with others' does transformation become possible.

> Only once we become more dissatisfied with our own reactive patterns than we are with others' does transformation become possible.

Earned secure attachment is possible because neuroscience proves that the more we practice something, the stronger we condition ourselves to it. This same principle explains why we are in our current state. We've already been practicing something, and those things that are maladaptive have become our current default in that area. The good news is, with intention and repetition, new, healthier patterns can take root and become our new default. Struggle is guaranteed, but as my friends Milan and Kay say, "Pick your pain. The pain of growth or the pain of staying stuck."

I hope you'll come along on this journey of getting unstuck and earning a secure attachment. So many have found freedom in it, and I believe you can too!

Marc

Understanding Your Attachment Style

Step One

Develop Insight

> Until you make the unconscious conscious,
> it will direct your life and you will call it fate.
> Attributed to Carl Jung

When the *Pokémon Go* craze peaked, my kids were young and did not have cell phones and we did not have unlimited data plans. So, my wife and I scheduled limited times each week for our kids to play the game on our cell phones. The month we downloaded this app we drained our data allowance at an unusually higher-than-normal rate; however, we did not make the correlation between the game and the data usage since we had been monitoring our kids' use of our phones.

I called our cell phone provider to figure out what was going on, convinced the problem must be on their end. The friendly customer service associate walked me through how to check some settings on my phone. An important element for *Pokémon Go* to be played is for the game to track your real-time geographic location. I learned that when our kids would launch the app to play, a pop-up notification would ask,

2   Understanding Your Attachment Style

"Allow *Pokémon Go* to use your location?" Instead of choosing "Allow while using app," they chose "Always allow," and unbeknownst to us, *Pokémon Go* was tracking our locations 24/7!

Equipped with this knowledge, I changed the setting and set up some data usage alerts. From then on, whenever I received a data limit notification that appeared unusual, the first thing I checked was this app setting. Prior to being aware of this, I was helpless to change what I did not know about. But once aware, I had the power to take control.

If you are not consciously aware of what drives your thinking and behaviors, you will be stuck like we were with the *Pokémon Go* game: knowing something is wrong, but helpless to change your settings. You can only control conscious behaviors. Though the terms "unconscious" and "subconscious" are often used interchangeably, technically, things in the unconscious mind are less recognizable to us because they are repressed, while the subconscious is just below conscious thought and can more easily become known if it's pointed out.

> You can only control conscious behaviors.

Only when you know how and why you are reacting can you stop it. Until then, you might not like your reactions and emotions that get stirred, but you will be limited in what you can do about them.

Like finding an app that's been running in the background, step one is about making the *sub*conscious *conscious*, so you can finally do something about it.

Chapter One

How We Attach (or Don't)

"Babe," I holler to my wife from the kitchen as I'm searching for food in the refrigerator. "I don't think we have anything here to eat. Should we go to the grocery store or order takeout?"

Hunger is driving my search for food. What I'm currently doing is not getting my need met, so I'm assessing my options. You've probably done the same countless times, I'm sure. Once I get food, my hunger will resolve, and I'll stop searching.

Emotions also drive our behaviors in an attempt to get our needs met. Just like food resolves the hunger feeling, each emotion has a corresponding need for it to resolve as well. These are not always as obvious, so how do you know what the need is for each emotion? Emotional needs can be determined by considering: What would I need more of to feel less of that emotion? If a child is fearful, her emotional need is for safety. Safety resolves fear, because the safer you feel, the less fearful you are. If a person is worried, his emotional need is for reassurance, because the more reassured you are, the less you worry. When someone is distressed, they need comfort, because the more comforted you feel, the less distressed you are. Hopefully, you're catching on. I've provided a list at the end of the book to help.

Our behaviors are the means to try and get our needs met, so here's my definition of emotional intelligence: the ability to observe and understand the emotion driving a behavior and the corresponding need it's trying to get met. For instance, if a person is yelling, he feels unheard, and needs to be heard. When a person is overexplaining, she feels misunderstood, and needs to be understood. When our emotional needs are consistently met by another, we feel attuned to them, and form a secure bond. However, if emotional needs go *unmet*, or worse, unnoticed, we develop self-protective coping strategies to compensate. These strategies are not inherently bad; they're adaptations given the perceived options available from what we've learned, though they don't often create relational closeness. For example: Pouting for attention, numbing, withdrawing, or lashing out are all common temporary coping methods for deeper unmet needs in relationships. (See Appendix for a chart on this.)

> When our emotional needs are consistently met by another, we feel attuned to them, and form a secure bond.

Each insecure attachment style has common core emotional wounds, and learned self-protective coping strategies to deal with the corresponding needs going unmet. Therefore, to understand how attachment forms, we need to understand the importance of being able to accurately identify emotions and corresponding needs.

> Each insecure attachment style has common core emotional wounds.

More About Attunement

Attunement is the ability to pick up on the thoughts or true underlying feelings of another person, as well as being willing to respond with care and attentiveness. It's like tuning into a radio station by knowing the correct frequency. When someone consistently "gets" you in this way, it brings a deep sense of comfort, connection, and emotional security in the relationship. Attunement is a learned skill, and people who have it are emotionally intelligent.

By observing the attunement between a child and her parent, attachment researchers can assess how securely that child is bonded to her caregiver even before she is one year old. An attuned parent can step outside their own perspective to see a situation through the child's eyes. This is how some parents understand a dark room can cause a child to feel vulnerable and anxious about imagined monsters and give them a night light or stay with them until they fall asleep. Less attuned parents might dismiss a child's fears by saying, "Go to sleep. There's nothing to worry about. Monsters aren't real."

Attunement doesn't try to change another's emotions. It accepts and *reflects* the emotions, showing understanding and empathy, in a *corresponding* way.

Responsiveness and attunement are not the same thing. Attunement follows an accurate understanding of what another feels and needs. For instance, giving a crying baby a bottle of milk could be a caring response. But if the baby is crying because she needs a diaper change, this response is mis-attuned.

Being mis-attuned does not mean the parent isn't trying their best. Often, when a person is in distress, we unintentionally focus on our own emotions rather than theirs. Instead of meeting their needs, we respond in a way that eases our own discomfort at seeing them feeling bad. If we tell them not to worry, offer to help cheer them up, or suggest a solution to their problem to feel like we've "done something," without genuinely understanding their emotions, while we have responded, it's not an attuned response because it's not what they needed. Emotions are uncomfortable and often irrational, so we can prefer to focus on encouraging logic and reason to try and get them to resolve. However, reason alone does not resolve emotions because the part of the brain that experiences emotions can be disconnected to time, language, or logic. This is why you may hear people who have intense emotional experiences describe events that last only a few seconds as feeling like an eternity or happening in slow motion. And they may describe being at a loss for words or knowing their feelings don't make logical sense.

If caregivers are not attuned, over time children learn they can't trust their needs will be met by them, and an insecure attachment style is developed as a self-protective coping strategy to deal with unmet needs. These habits of relating begin so early in life, they become ingrained and often operate subconsciously, forming patterns that carry into adulthood.

What Secure Attachment Means

Three-year-old Elijah is running toward a slide at the park. Hitting a hidden tree root, Elijah falls face-first into the mulch covering the hard ground. He begins to let out a cry.

"Sweetie," says his mother, watching from a nearby bench. "Did you fall? Come here."

Sobbing, Elijah stumbles over to his mother.

"Where does it hurt, honey?" she asks. "Is it your knees?"

Looking together at his knees, she brushes off pieces of mulch.

"Is it your hands?" she asks with concern.

Together they brush off his hands.

"I'm so sorry you fell. I understand why you feel like crying. Can I hold you?"

Nodding, Elijah climbs up onto his mother's lap.

While his mother feels his sadness, she's comforted to know he enjoys the cuddle as much as she does. She notices him relaxing into her, and after a few minutes he pushes himself up.

"Can I play?" he asks.

"Okay. I'm glad you feel better now."

The child who grows up with a secure attachment has an attuned parent who recognizes and reflects their internal state, empathizes with their emotions, asks about and validates their feelings, and meets needs in a corresponding way. I know all this can seem like a lot to consider doing *every time* a child has big feelings! And this is why it's so often impaired, partial, or missing altogether. The secure parent is not perfect, but they respond more often than not in appropriately supportive ways, accepting and helping the child manage even difficult emotions like fear, jealousy, and anger. As a result, the child learns emotions are shareable and bearable.

Being accepting of all emotions doesn't mean approving of all behaviors or perspectives—we'll cover more on that later. Yet when a child in distress has help managing their emotions from an attuned parent, the child feels understood, seen, and loved. And the next time they experience distress (or positive feelings), they'll likely go back to that parent to share this, knowing their feelings will be accepted.

Emotions Are Either Talked Out or Acted Out

When children aren't taught the language to express their feelings clearly and accurately, they act them out hoping a parent will understand. In times of distress, this takes the form of protest behavior, designed to get the parent's attention, hoping the parent will see their need and help. Think about how you might communicate your needs with someone who speaks a different language. You rely on universal gestures to help them understand what your words are not conveying. Children do the same, but in childlike ways, such as sulking, pouting, withdrawing, or yelling. This is why developing accurate emotional vocabulary to verbalize feelings is paramount to becoming a securely attached adult. Because if you don't ever learn language to communicate your emotions, you will continue to act them out.

Emotional vocabulary helps us put words to our inner experiences, giving us language to describe how events in our history have impacted us. This, in turn, allows us to build a coherent narrative to explain how we have been shaped. Most parents do the best they can with the knowledge they have learned. But by knowing how you felt growing up and what you needed, and seeing what you did to deal with these needs going unmet, you can begin to build your coherent narrative.

One family posted five simple drawings of faces expressing various emotions near their breakfast table. The pictures were labeled: "happy," "sad," "mad," "worried," and "afraid." During meals, and especially as their young children talked about what was happening in their worlds, the parents pointed to the pictures and asked the child to choose which one he or she was feeling. What these parents were doing was helping their children build coherent narratives in the present to make sense of their inner emotions. Before they could read, these children understood the joyful happy face, the tearful sad face, the fiery angry face, the anxious worried face, and the distressed scared face. They were given the tools to put words to their feelings and know they were okay to express.

Facial charts are how young children learn about emotions because children learn to read facial expressions and tone of voice long before language. A baby might coo when a parent plays peekaboo with them, but if the infant starts to feel hungry and cry, then an attuned parent will change their expression to mirror the baby's pursed, crying lips. The parent may say soothing words while getting the bottle ready: "Oh, you're hungry! You want to say it's time to feed you! I'll get your bottle ready." While the baby does not understand the language, they notice the change in expression and tone that indicate their need is recognized.

Learning how to express our emotions and communicate our needs through appropriate language reduces the need to act them out. However, insecure attachments lack language to share emotional states effectively and request for needs appropriately. As a result, these individuals resort to dramatized protests or defensive reactions hoping others will guess their needs or back down.

Think of attachment as relationship programming. How well a parent can relate to his or her child will determine how well that child is programmed to relate to others.

Thanks to Elijah's fall at the park, and his mother's attunement and comfort, he's well on his way to learning to self-soothe when he faces times of distress and doesn't have his mother nearby to help. Similarly, as we grow and leave home as adults, we're more secure when we can recognize and manage our emotions. Children with secure attachments form the belief: "My parents understand and comfort me and help me feel better. My emotions matter, and I can express them confidently and manage them. I trust others can do the same for me, and I'm able to do it for them."

> We're more secure when we can recognize and manage our emotions.

Such confidence comes from consistent attunement, and that creates secure attachment.

The Five Insecure Attachment Styles

British psychologist John Bowlby was the first attachment theorist. He made his initial observations in the mid-1930s. But it wasn't until later, while working in a psychiatric hospital, that he differentiated between two different reactions in children who were facing separation from their parents. He observed some children were distant and emotionless as they dealt with the stress, while others clung tightly to prevent the parent leaving. After being separated, the second group actively searched for their parents and protested—crying, throwing tantrums, and refusing to eat. Bowlby noted there was an "anxious-avoidant spectrum" in insecure attachment behavior.[*]

Eventually, Mary Ainsworth, an American Canadian psychologist, and her colleagues advanced Bowlby's theories through her "Strange

---

[*] John Bowlby, *Attachment and Loss* (Hogarth Press, 1969).

Situation" study in 1969. These experiments measured how children between the ages of twelve and eighteen months old reacted to being separated from and reunited with their mothers. It's called the "Strange Situation" because the experiment also measured the child's reactions to a stranger both in and out of their mother's presence. In the study, eight events were observed in three minutes: 1) Mother and infant are left to play together with toys in a room, then 2) a stranger enters, and 3) mother greets the stranger and briefly interacts with her. Next, 4) mother leaves, and the infant is left alone with the stranger. Before long, 5) mother returns and the stranger leaves. After that, 6) mother leaves, and this time, 7) the stranger returns without the mother. Then, 8) mother returns.

At each point, Ainsworth wanted to observe the children's differences in separation anxiety, stranger anxiety, reunion behavior, and willingness to explore. From these experiments, she identified another distinction within insecure-anxious attachment—an anxious-resistant style. "Anxious-resistant" children demonstrated intense distress when the mother left but were also resistant to their mother's comfort when reunited. Several years later in 1986, Mary Main, one of Ainsworth's students, continuing the same experiments, identified a "disorganized" style. When distressed, these infants seemed not to know whether to run toward their mother for comfort or away for relief.*

This early research helped to define the types of insecure attachment—**Avoider, Pleaser, Vacillator, Controller**, and **Victim** styles, with the Controller and Victim styles forming from disorganized attachment. While these aren't the traditional terms, I will use them because they more clearly highlight the key characteristic

---

* Mary D. Salter Ainsworth, Mary C. Blehar, Everett Waters, and Sally N. Wall, *Patterns of Attachment: A Psychological Study of the Strange Situation* (Psychology Press, 2015).

of each style, as described in Milan and Kay Yerkovich's book, *How We Love*.*

These reactions form in children based on how primary caregivers behave when the child is distressed. Parents' attachment styles influence the child's attachment style, but attachment styles aren't simply "passed down." Sometimes, a style develops from coping strategies used to deal with circumstances beyond a parent's control, such as a large family with multiple siblings all in need of a parent's attention, a parent's untraditional work schedule that makes the parent intermittently unavailable, the unexpected death of a parent, a premature birth, the child being hospitalized, or a chronically sick or disabled sibling. Life challenges and many other factors complicate how we form connections.

Let's take a brief look at how the insecure primary styles develop.

The Avoider Attachment Style

Not long after Elijah fell, Jackson, another child, took a tumble. Without any tenderness, his mother simply instructed him, "Jackson, you're okay. Stop crying," dismissing Jackson's painful experience altogether, and giving him the message of "you're feeling too much."

Even seemingly more reassuring phrases such as "It's okay. Be brave," or "Don't worry, it's going to be fine!" discourage expressing emotions. The child who receives these messages learns their parent is not able to help manage their emotions in the way they need. Because emotions lead to needs, over time, this child's most adaptive self-protective strategy becomes to suppress and avoid their emotions so as to not have needs. They form an Avoider attachment style.

Dismissiveness and discomfort with showing affection are probably the most common signs of avoidant attachment. The parent with

---

*   Milan Yerkovich and Kay Yerkovich, *How We Love: A Revolutionary Approach to Deeper Connections in Marriage* (WaterBrook Press, 2017).

this style unknowingly communicates the message to their child that emotions are signs of being too needy. Of course, many of these parents don't realize they are giving this message and likely had Avoider parents of their own or formed dismissive strategies due to life circumstances causing them to be independent before they should have. The vast majority of these parents never intend to leave children to think they are alone to figure things out for themselves. Many believe they are raising resilient kids by teaching them to quickly get over their emotions.

I know parenting is the most difficult job in the world. I am one who has made many mistakes myself. Yet an Avoider style most often develops from a lack of emotional connection and tenderness in childhood. Avoider parents emphasize responsibility, task mastery, and self-reliance for the child. They typically are performance-oriented, offering approval only when the child succeeds or can provide for themselves. Emotional suppression becomes automatic, causing the child developing an Avoider attachment style to become unaware of their own emotions.

The Pleaser Attachment Style
A third child at the park, Kara, was playing on the jungle gym within her father's sight but kept running back to check in with him to make sure she wasn't doing anything wrong.

During her play, her father called to her several times. "Kara, you're getting too far away," when she went to the slide on the far end of the playground, and "Kara, play where I can see you," when she disappeared into the tubes on the jungle gym. A group of older children not accompanied by adults showed up, and Kara's father beckoned her to come back to the bench he was on. "Let those big kids play now. I don't want you to get in their way or you could get hurt."

Feeling anxious by her father's worry, Kara scooted close to him. When a parent is overprotective and hypervigilant to danger, the child cannot explore with confidence. The child receives the message that the world is dangerous, and to stay close to keep safe. Exploration is limited, and they learn not to trust their own sense for danger.

Children with this style monitor their parent's mood to keep their parent calm and reduce the anxiety they feel when their parent is stressed.

Chronically angry, critical, or depressed parents can also cause a child to develop a Pleaser attachment style. Either the parent's anger frightens the child, or the parent's criticism and high expectations make the child feel incompetent, or the child caretakes the parent. Similarly, rescuing or smothering a child so they don't experience any type of challenge sends the message they're not capable, causing a lack of confidence and individuality. Without encouragement to take normal risks, the child's emotional development is put behind managing the parent's emotions. This child develops fears, anxiety, clinginess, or performance anxiety.

The Pleaser's self-protective strategy is to placate others to keep their own anxiety at bay.

The Vacillator Attachment Style
Sarah and her babysitter had arrived at the park, with the promise that Sarah's mother would meet them there. Two hours later, when Sarah's mother was still busy with work obligations, Sarah had grown tired, and the pair returned home.

When Sarah's mother got home that night, just a few minutes before Sarah's bedtime, Sarah refused to make eye contact with her mother.

"I brought you a squishy ball from my meeting today," her mother offered, feeling guilty.

Sarah didn't answer, pouting because she was sad that she had not seen her mother all day and now she had to go to sleep. Sarah's mother felt hurt that Sarah did not accept the gift and said, "Okay, you look like you want me to leave you alone. Maybe you'll be ready to talk to me tomorrow," and she left Sarah to get in bed by herself.

> Inconsistent connection from a caregiver can encourage a Vacillator attachment style.

Abandonment or inconsistent connection from a caregiver can encourage a Vacillator attachment style. This child wants connection but is abandoned or left to wait until the parent is ready or available. The child protests by dramatizing their hurt feelings for the parent to notice and come and soothe them, yet when the parent does come close, the child pushes away or struggles to be comforted. This is the anxious-resistant style identified by Mary Ainsworth. The child feels anxious, unseen, lonely, and misunderstood. They want the parent to know, "I want your attention, but I'm upset you make me wait for it!"

The child vacillates between feeling good when enjoying connection and feeling bad when it suddenly disappears. Frequent absences or limited enjoyable connection leaves the child longing for more. Sometimes intermittent connection is beyond a parent's control, from working rotating schedules, travelling for work, or serving in the military. Divorce and shared custody are common contributors to a child having intermittent connection with a parent.

Without language to express emotions, children have little choice but to try whatever their temperament leans toward—pouting or tantrums—to get their parent's attention. The parent's undependability creates the struggle in the child between longing to be seen and understood in their distress, craving connection when it is available, and anxiety that it may disappear again soon. The Vacillator's self-protective strategy is to protest to get others to notice their hurt and then to push away to be in control of the disconnection and reduce the abandonment feeling.

The Controller and Victim Attachment Styles

Anamaria and her little brother had brought toy trucks to the park and were creating racetracks in the dirt behind the small building that housed the restrooms. Their mother, who stayed in her car to get high, couldn't see them from the parking lot.

A group of teenage boys ducked behind the building to smoke marijuana. Anamaria felt uncomfortable but continued to play because she knew her brother was having fun.

When the boys began to trail away, one remained. He put his hand up Anamaria's dress and touched her beneath her underwear. He then exposed himself to her, before running off and laughing.

In the moment she froze, not knowing what she should do. After the boy left, she considered running to her mother to report the incident. But she had reported a similar incident that occurred with one of her mother's boyfriends, and her mother had blamed her for looking.

Frequently, children who suffer some kind of abuse wind up with a Controller or Victim attachment style. They usually can't depend on their parent for safety, let alone comfort. The parent is either physically, emotionally, or sexually abusive; or neglectful, exposing the child to these dangers.

Both these styles fall under the "**disorganized**" **attachment** identified by Mary Main, in which children engage in "approach-avoid" behavior. The instinct to *run from* danger conflicts with the drive to *run toward* a protective attachment in their parent. Chaotic or neglectful homes leave children in unsolvable predicaments when the ones who should be providing care and safety do not, and are themselves a source of danger. These children have fright without solutions. Meeting needs is reduced to survival, and these children may try all the other insecure self-protective strategies, with mixed results. Sometimes this is because they have various caregivers with different attachment styles in multiple foster homes. As a result, a combination of insecure attachment styles may develop, which is referred to as "disorganized."

In prolonged trauma, this style can split into one of two main expressions: a passive Victim who freezes and disassociates, or a Controller who learns to fight back and dominate others to control their environment. Controllers are hypervigilant to threats that trigger shame of being made to feel weak again. Controller children might play out their trauma at school, but becoming the abuser they face at home, while Victim children are vulnerable to being sexually abused or bullied by others. In chaotic homes, unpredictability means danger. The Controller's dominant self-protective strategy is to control others through intimidation and threats, so relationships are never unpredictable again. Victims learn they cannot stop the abuse, so their self-protective strategy is to remain small and invisible to reduce the frequency of it.

Why Attachment Styles Matter

As you think about your own childhood and the style that feels most familiar to you now, your parents' approach may not fit exactly into one particular style, or they may have grown as you got older. Yet understanding what secure attachment is and how the insecure styles form is essential to understanding how we can attach securely in adult relationships.

Next, we'll look at how early in life bonds get formed, and how even experiences as babies that we can't remember can affect our adult lives.

REFLECT

1. What did you notice about how you relate to others *today*? Do you verbalize your emotions securely or dramatize your emotions insecurely?

2. As you read this chapter, what childhood memories did you recall? What insights—into yourself or others—did you glean?

3. What confirmed something you already knew about yourself or others?

4. What attachment styles did your parents have when you were growing up? While reading, what attachment style resonated for you or as the one you may be instilling in your children?

5. What insights did you gain from reflecting on how your parents raised you, with what you know about your grandparents, and how your parents' own attachment styles developed?

Chapter Two

The Cycle of Bonding

Emily and her eighteen-month-old daughter, Avery, are at a playdate at a friend's house. While the moms chat over coffee in the living room, their toddlers play nearby. Feeling comfortable enough to explore, Avery wanders away from her mother's side and follows the other toddler into the adjoining playroom, out of sight.

After a minute or so, Avery runs back to the living room to check if her mother is still there.

Emily smiles. "Are you having fun exploring?"

Avery giggles and runs back into the playroom. This repeats several times with Avery building confidence to spend a few more minutes each time in the playroom before returning to where she left her mother. Avery is learning to trust her mother's consistent availability even when she is out of sight. This is called "object constancy." Avery also is learning she can return to her mother for safety and comfort if she needs to.

Trust, safety, and affection from our caregivers, or the lack thereof, is the infrastructure for how we learn to form relationships in what's called the cycle of bonding. This is the foundation of attachment. When an infant bonds with her caregivers, she is determining through

> The cycle of bonding is the foundation of attachment.

their interactions whether she can trust them to understand her cries and provide for her basic needs. As she grows into early childhood, she explores to the edge of her comfort zone. If the parent has established safe limits, the child will venture out a little further each time and develop self-confidence and autonomy while also knowing they can return for instruction, encouragement, comfort, and soothing. Avery's mother's consistency and safety as a *secure base* is forming a template for Avery for how to build secure attachments to others in the world.

However, if a parent is fearful or controlling, and limits exploration, the child becomes anxious and does not develop the self-confidence and autonomy needed for secure attachment. Babies have little ability to soothe themselves, and they need a parent to hold, rock, and gently talk to them when they are distressed. When a parent is unable to attune to their child and meet their needs, or soothe them, the child is conditioned for insecure attachment.

Because babies' communication is prelinguistic and mainly nonverbal, they look for their parent to mirror their facial expressions to know they are being understood. Born with one hundred billion neurons (brain cells) but relatively few synaptic connections (the wiring that joins these brain cells together), babies' brains are estimated to make one million new connections *per second* from birth to age two. And for the first three years of life, studies show a predominance of blood flow in the right hemisphere of the brain, the side believed to be responsible for emotional development. Language is needed for narrative memory of events, so during the preverbal years (0–2) when the areas of the brain responsible for language and perception of the self in time are still developing, the memories a baby forms are wordless. These are called implicit memories and are emotional and bodily feeling in nature. A baby's brain can wire together a parent's smile with an emotion of safety and a bodily feeling of ease, or they can wire together a parent's angry or worried face with an emotion of fear and a tense bodily feeling.

So, if you think babies are too young to remember an interaction or event, they in fact do. However, it's in an implicit feeling memory, rather than in explicit story memory. With this understanding, we can see that we arrive in the world biologically ready to be programmed for emotional connection as the primary way to build a relationship.

Children who are consistently soothed by their caregivers begin to develop an internal template for how to self-soothe. In contrast, children who are not soothed often grow up with nervous systems that are easily dysregulated and struggle to calm themselves. Without intervention, this conditioning carries into adulthood. Through their early connections with caregivers, children form mental representations as their core beliefs about whether the world is safe and others are trustworthy. These foundational beliefs shape how they approach and experience relationships throughout life.

The Stages of Development

In 1950, Erik Erikson, a German American developmental psychologist, identified stages of psychosocial development from infancy through adulthood, which he believed individuals must complete to achieve healthy personality and avoid identity crisis.[*] He theorized these stages build upon one another, so failure to complete earlier stages would impact the ability to complete later stages.

Infancy (0–1 years)—Trust vs. Mistrust

Through attunement, responsiveness, and nurturing, the baby learns whether others can be trusted to meet their needs and form meaningful bonds with. However, if the parent is mis-attuned, neglectful, unaffectionate, or inconsistent, the baby learns others can't be trusted to meet their needs and may become anxious, suspicious, and untrusting.

---

[*]   Erik H. Erikson, *Childhood and Society* (Norton, 1950).

Early childhood (1–3 years)—Autonomy vs. Shame and Doubt
The parent supports the child to try self-care and other tasks by himself with supervision until he succeeds or until the child asks for assistance, and the child learns autonomy and self-control that lead to healthy self-esteem and willpower. However, when a parent limits, discourages, shows disappointment in, or shames the child's efforts in this stage, the child may learn poor self-control, doubt their abilities, shame themselves, or develop low self-esteem.

Preschool (3–6 years)—Initiative vs. Guilt
The parent encourages exploration of the child's likes, and the child develops self-directed behavior, goal formation, sense of purpose, and agency in her environment as she plans activities, accomplishes tasks, and faces challenges. However, if the parent discourages initiative or criticizes efforts, there may be a lack of self-initiated behavior or guilt over failed efforts.

School Age (6–12 years)—Industry vs. Inferiority
The parent encourages the child to develop his skills, and he gains a sense of competency and belief in his abilities. However, if the parent harshly criticizes or restricts the child from developing and demonstrating his skills, the child may lack confidence in his ability and develop a sense of inferiority.

Adolescence (12–20 years)—Identity vs. Role Confusion
The parent supports the adolescent in searching for her place in the world, and she feels free to explore her individuality and identity separate from the parent and develops a strong sense of self. However, when the parent does not give this space to explore, confusion about personal identity and where she fits in with groups can result.

Young Adult (20–35 years)—Intimacy vs. Isolation
The young adult who has learned how to securely attach with others is able to create intimacy and fulfillment in committed, reciprocal relationships. However, young adults with an insecure attachment will struggle with intimacy, and could come to feel isolated, detached, and/or experience significant fear of rejection, leading to broken relationships.

When a child's care is sufficiently affirming, comforting, and consistent, children can draw upon these many experiences to self-soothe in times of stress, confident there are others in the world who are safe and secure to help them. When this doesn't adequately occur, a child forms self-protective coping strategies and an insecure connection with themselves and others. And this is what leads to developing one of the insecure attachment styles.

Does Culture Influence Attachment?

Let's take a brief moment to comment about the impact of culture on attachment. Some cultures (and religious subcultures) can be more avoidant and less expressive, or more reliant upon needs being met as a collective than we tend to associate with secure attachment. This does tend to influence people of these cultures to be more insecurely attached, even though it is the cultural norm for most people to act this way. Cultures that provide a strong emphasis on individualism may see a higher prevalence of avoidant attachments, while cultures that promote collectivism may see a higher prevalence of anxious attachments. While different cultures may vary in their emotional displays, a few basic emotions appear to be universal. Culture is an environmental factor, not an intrinsic trait. Attachment style development is also shaped environmentally, derived from our caregivers' responsiveness to us, yet how bonding occurs in humans is the same regardless of culture or race. Overcoming some cultural conditioning is then often necessary to achieve healthy emotional connections.

> So, the question is, if we didn't get what we needed from our caregivers or society, what do we do?

So, the question is, if we didn't get what we needed from our caregivers or society, what do we do?

Reprogramming for Attunement

If we did not receive parental attunement in childhood—with recognition, acceptance, validation, and empathy for our feelings—we likely won't have the internal template needed to engage in the full cycle of bonding with others. We then need to learn and practice the skills required to create secure attachments in adulthood. To do this work, you will need at least one secure base—someone who has a secure attachment who can offer you consistent support and emotional safety—much like the sense of security a child develops with a trusted parent as their safe reference. Only through a reparative experience can you build new neural pathways for secure connection. This can happen in therapy with a therapist serving as your attuned attachment figure or with a coach, teacher, pastor, or mentor who can affirm, comfort, and appropriately challenge you. Spouses can also become secure bases for one another by taking turns to practice attuning. I'm going to show you an interaction between a husband and wife who *didn't* receive what they needed as children to effectively communicate with each other but who were willing to practice some skills together to get unstuck.

Craig and Jan came to me exasperated. Neither felt like the other made efforts to understand them. Craig wanted to talk problems through, but he would become animated and raise his voice to get his point across when he didn't feel like Jan was listening to him. As a quieter child, Jan grew up in a home of "yellers." She wanted to avoid any drama and so did not have the capacity to listen to Craig when he got worked up. His emotional intensity was so often out of proportion to events, it seemed logical to her that he was the problem. Yet Craig felt dismissed when Jan told him to "calm down," and that he was "overreacting," and his frustration only intensified. Eventually, they would arrive at a stalemate, both retreating in hurt with no resolution. This is how we began therapy.

In our second session together, I introduced the "Comfort Circle." This is a format for a structured conversation developed by Milan and Kay Yerkovich, where there are two clearly defined roles: a listener and a speaker. Using thoughtful and engaging questions, the listener shows their intention to understand the speaker's experience. They help the speaker resolve their emotions through demonstrating empathy and offering to meet the emotional need. Since this was their first time, I coached them through the conversation. While in the speaker role Craig identified his top three emotions about their latest conflict as "disappointed," "rejected," and "mocked" when Jan had walked away. Jan, who was following my prompts, instead of defending or explaining, asked how often Craig felt that way. "Every day," he said. She then asked Craig if he remembered feeling this way as a child, and after a moment Craig's eyes welled up. Now that Craig wasn't fighting in anger to be heard, he was able to be more reflective and vulnerable.

"When I was sixteen, I waited by a girl's car after school with a handmade sign to ask her to prom. She said no and drove off and I quickly left too feeling disappointed and embarrassed. However, word got around quickly, and other kids mocked me relentlessly. For the rest of that year, she also avoided me."

"Did you think she liked you?" Jan inquired further.

Craig stared at the carpet. "I thought she did. We had worked together in a group one time and a couple of other times she asked to borrow a pen from me. I thought there was more of a chance she would say yes or I wouldn't have asked. The worst part was because our school was small, she and I had homeroom together, and I had to see her almost every day after that."

Having to see this girl every day after she rejected him explains why Craig experienced those same emotions with Jan *every day*. Being quickly dismissed in the parking lot and then being teased by his peers explained why Craig's feelings of rejection and being mocked were connected with his feeling of disappointment when Jan left too. Our impressionable brains wire together connections from our experiences—situations, people, places, feelings—and then create a shortcut for a neural pathway by associating them all together. Then when any one of these elements are present, we get reminded of the others from the old experience. Until we get new corrective experiences, unprocessed memories—especially negative ones—will likely shape our present expectations, causing us to project past outcomes as the "likeliest" result for similar situations. Through understanding how this significant past experience was impacting his present, Craig and Jan were able to finally understand and depersonalize Craig's feelings and reactions toward Jan. Jan's new awareness helped her better tune into why Craig felt emotions so strongly during their disagreements. And Craig soon learned to decouple his old emotions from the present and stop blaming Jan for his perception of her rejecting and dismissing him.

I've seen many amazing insights like this occur for people simply by asking them to take a few moments to reflect on their history.

Three Ways to Listen Effectively

Defining listener and speaker roles and learning to take turns is fundamental to communicating effectively. It's in these defined roles that individuals can learn to speak in a way to encourage listening—by using "I" statements and limiting absolutes ("always," "never")—and listen in a way that invites others to open up.

Effective listening is more than just staying silent and letting another person talk. It involves a few specific skills. Individuals with learned secure attachment usually had a parent who knew how to listen in the following ways.

Attentive Listening

Attentive listening employs body language that shows you are listening by facing the speaker and making eye contact, leaning forward, nodding along as they talk, and making affirming sounds so the speaker *sees* you are listening. Individuals with secure attachments know the value of body language and are aware that much is being communicated nonverbally. They don't shake their head, roll their eyes, or sigh, which shuts down sharing vulnerably.

Active Listening

Active listening means fully engaging with what someone is saying by asking thoughtful, relevant questions to better understand their perspective. When you do this, the speaker *knows* you are listening because you are directly interacting with what they are saying. Secure individuals can thoughtfully dialogue, knowing that considering another's viewpoint doesn't mean they are giving in or losing theirs. Securely attached people tolerate hearing things they may not like or agree with.

Reflective Listening

Reflective listening involves repeating key words or phrases from the speaker to confirm they've been heard and understood. In addition, the listener mirrors the speaker's emotional state by offering empathy and validating feelings based on *the speaker's viewpoint*. When you do these things, the speaker *feels* listened to. Securely attached people are aware that showing understanding is not the same as agreeing.

Here's a technique I developed that incorporates the three important listening skills to improve conversations in an easy-to-remember three-step process. I call it **"Reflect-Connect-Respond."**

First Reflect—repeat back or summarize what the speaker is saying: *"I hear you saying..."*

Then Connect—use a validating or empathetic statement to connect with the speaker's emotional experience. This bridges the gap between what they've said and how you are going to respond to it. Validating affirms you understand the way they see it, or you agree with some of their perspective, or their feelings make sense and matter to you. (*"That makes sense,"* or *"I can understand how you would feel that way..."*) Empathy shows you can relate to how that emotion affects them. (*"That sounds painful,"* or *"That must have been difficult for you."*) Connecting is the most important step in this process. Sometimes, just connecting to someone's pain is all that's needed for comfort or resolution or to encourage continued sharing.

Now Respond—after reflecting what you heard and connecting with the speaker's emotion, it's time to respond to what was said by asking a thoughtful question to find out more or letting them know if you can meet their needs. However, don't use questions to "lead the witness" or justify your actions. This is not about sharing your perspective yet.

> Sometimes, just connecting to someone else's pain is all that's needed for comfort or resolution or to encourage continued sharing.

Repeat the process as needed until you understand and have fully heard them out, or their emotion subsides. If you don't know what someone needs, ask, but also be mindful that every emotion has a *corresponding* need and people don't always make this connection with their requests. If others are unsure, help them connect their emotions to the corresponding need.

Here's what that might sound like:

"I'm hearing you feel misunderstood, and you need me to understand."
"You feel unheard and need me to hear you."
"You feel sad and need comfort."
"You feel worried and need reassurance."
"You feel wronged and need an apology and a promise from me to try to do things differently next time."

As you learn to "Reflect-Connect-Respond" you will see this is far more effective than the typical stating facts, defending actions, and blaming the other person for your hurts, which often leads to conflict.

Consider this conversation between a husband and wife to see how this can play out in an everyday interaction:

Shortly after arriving home a husband inquires of his wife, "You seem quiet. How did your job interview go?" He's observing her mood and *reflecting* what he is seeing.

Seeming conflicted, she answers, "I'm not sure. I thought I prepared well, but I got stuck on a couple of questions."

The husband *reflecting* says, "Oh, the questions caught you off guard."

Feeling seen, the wife answers, "Right. I should have prepared better."

Continuing to *reflect*, the husband takes a guess at his wife's emotions: "Sounds like you are feeling disappointed in yourself."

"I am," his wife responds.

Now *connecting* with his wife through validating her feelings, the husband affirms, "I know you prepared hard for this, and you are excited about this position. I can see why you are disappointed."

Then, *responding* with comfort, he touches her hand and adds, "I'm sorry. I know you are a dedicated employee, and they would be lucky to have you join their team." He *responds* again by offering support:

"Would you like me to help you write a 'Thank you' email for the interview or look at some strategies for improvement?"

Ambivalent, his wife answers, "Maybe...I don't know if I want to do that now, though."

"Okay," he *responds*. "I'm here if you need my help. I love you and I think you are amazing!"

I suspect this is the kind of interaction you would *welcome* after a bad experience. It's a technique I frequently walk couples through, and it's amazing how many people report feeling better hearing their spouse give these attuned responses, even when they know they were coached. If you find that you often get stuck arguing, learn to "Reflect-Connect-Respond." It's powerful!

Why It Matters

Understanding what you missed in the cycle of bonding as a child, and noticing where your current relationships are struggling, can help you admit relational deficits. It might not be easy to admit where you struggle, let alone to accept the effort it will take to employ healthy communication skills. Yet from my experience personally and with clients in applying this material, as well as the accounts of so many people who have done the work of earning secure attachment, I'm convinced nothing will help you better understand and resolve your recurring conflict patterns. If nothing else, practicing how to listen in this way will undoubtedly help you have more productive conversations. Whether or not you have a motivated partner on this journey with you, changing your part in a conflict pattern will help free you from your reflexive reactivity.

Here is the hope: Research shows that individuals who did not learn a secure attachment in childhood can recondition and "rewire" to learn and earn a secure attachment in adulthood. Even if you had a difficult childhood, the most important factor in earning secure attachment isn't the number or intensity of our adverse experiences. What matters most is how we come to make sense of our childhood experiences and whether we can create a coherent narrative of it. Everyone has emotional triggers. Those who are able to reflect on their childhoods, to understand how their triggers formed and acknowledge the reactive strategies they developed to self-protect, can begin to see these patterns as *learned* insecurities that can be overcome, rather than fixed traits. And this is where the exciting journey toward earning secure attachment begins.

In the coming chapters I want to help you discover your story to build your coherent narrative. For this process to be successful, you need to recognize, accept, and understand how insecurities formed in you and shaped your attachment. When you can do this, you will see how it impacts your perceptions of current relationships and subsequent reactions to try and get your core needs met. The journey of repairing the developmental stages you did not successfully complete in childhood begins as you create new experiences to override the old ones. With practice of self-exploration, you can learn to self-soothe and develop new secure strategies.

> What matters most is how we come to make sense of our childhood experiences and whether we can create a coherent narrative of it.

In fact, one of the best things you can do is understand how and why you react so you can learn to leave reactions in the past, and be responsive in the present. This is where we're going next.

REFLECT

1. How attuned were your parents to your emotions and how responsive were they to your needs during childhood?

2. How attuned and responsive are your spouse and/or parents to your emotions and needs now?

3. What childhood stages do you think you did not successfully complete? What hindered your progress?

4. Have you learned attentive, active, and reflective listening skills? Which ones do you need to grow in?

5. Can you identify someone who can be a secure base to affirm, comfort, and appropriately challenge you as you grow?

Chapter Three

Reprogramming the Amygdala

During a visit to his grandmother's house at age six, Oliver slipped out to the backyard to play with her new dog—a recent rescue from the shelter. Hoping to play fetch, he picked up a stick to throw for the dog, but the dog reacted unexpectedly. It charged at him, snarling and growling. Oliver froze in terror, too frightened to move or even call for help. Though his mother and grandmother rushed to his rescue in under a minute, the experience felt like an eternity to Oliver.

Even though he had loved and enjoyed playing with his grandmother's old dog, that single frightening moment left a lasting impact. Oliver developed a fear of dogs. From then on, even the sound of a bark, whether in real life or on TV, would trigger a surge of anxiety. He'd start to sweat and feel as though he were in immediate danger. Oliver avoided dogs whenever possible. He determined he would never be left alone with one again. From his experience, he formed powerful internal beliefs that "dogs can't be trusted" and "others might not be available to help when I need it."

When Oliver was twenty-six, he met Tara, his soon-to-be wife. She had a tiny Pomeranian named Pickles who would happily yap and run up to them every time they arrived at her house. While Tara saw Pickles as cute and harmless, Oliver would instinctively freeze, staying very still.

Tara found his hesitation a bit silly, not understanding why someone would be nervous around such a small dog. But for Oliver, his reaction was deeply ingrained. Staying still had once saved him and had kept him safe around dogs ever since.

Ever wondered why you or others overreact? The culprit is your amygdalae. There are two—one on each side of the brain, though most often referred to in the singular, as the amygdala. These almond-sized groups of neurons embedded in the middle of each brain hemisphere are small but *very* significant. It is believed our amygdala is the source of the predominant reactions—fight, flight, and freeze—that define each of the attachment styles' stress behaviors. So, understanding how your amygdala gets activated can be very helpful to earning secure attachment.

The amygdala is also our threat detection center. Most of our daily thought processes and decision-making are quarterbacked from the prefrontal cortex (the *PFC*, for short), and the amygdala plays a crucial role in processing and evaluating emotional information, especially negative emotions connected to people, places, and situations. The PFC is located behind your forehead and houses your executive thinking capabilities that are responsible for analytical reasoning, language, planning, and emotion regulation. The PFC is like your mission control tower where most daily decisions are run through...until you perceive a threat. That's when the amygdala takes over.

> When you perceive a threat, the amygdala takes over.

Since the amygdalae are so essential to our survival, they develop rapidly during postnatal life, and they literally hijack our brains and take control to give us split-second decision-making capability to save our lives. These reflex reactions occur faster than conscious thought—often triggered by fear or anger—processing information in milliseconds,*

---

* Yingying Wang et al., "Rapid Processing of Invisible Fearful Faces in the Human Amygdala," *Journal of Neuroscience* 43, no. 8 (2023): 1405–1413, https://www.jneurosci.org/content/43/8/1405.

before the PFC has time to assess the situation and overrule them, even when the threat isn't truly life-threatening.

In addition, the amygdala sends signals to other areas of the brain to deactivate nonessential functions during a perceived survival-level threat, while also sending signals to activate others it deems necessary for fight or flight or freeze behaviors. Our parasympathetic nervous system, responsible for "rest and digest" and "feed and breed" functions, shuts down, and our sympathetic nervous system, which puts our body on alert, activates. The heart beats faster to pump adrenaline and cortisol to large muscles, getting us ready to move, while our pupils dilate to take in as much information as possible about the threat. Like Oliver, most people have a story where this biological response helped save them at one time at least.

The amygdala assigns emotional significance to memories, and the more significant the event, the more acute and enduring the memory becomes. These are not detailed memories like a video recorder, but more tags of emotional components to people, events, and places. Since the amygdala develops quicker than the PFC,* which does not conclude development until around our midtwenties, it can serve as a biological tutor to the developing PFC, alarming at times when it is not needed due to these emotional tags. When triggered often in childhood, and without help to soothe, the amygdala can teach us to feel threatened even when there is no real danger. This is why children need a parent who has a fully developed brain to act as their PFC and help them regulate emotions, make sense of their experiences, and respond thoughtfully rather than reactively.

> The amygdala can teach us to feel threatened even when there is no real danger.

---

* Akiko Uematsu et al., "Developmental Trajectories of Amygdala and Hippocampus from Infancy to Early Adulthood in Healthy Individuals," *PLOS One* 7, no. 10 (2012), https://doi.org/10.1371/journal.pone.0046970.

An overly reactive amygdala that struggles to filter false positives will sound the alarm with high intensity each time, much like a smoke detector blares at the same volume whether you've burned the toast or the house is on fire.

What our amygdala assesses to be the most adaptive reaction in that moment determines whether we will fight, flight, or freeze. And because the amygdala is a learning system, first experiences shape future experiences. The more a neural pathway is reinforced, the more likely it will be followed again in the future.

This is why significant past experiences make perceived threats in the present feel bigger than they are and the reason Oliver continued his freeze response with Pickles, even though this dog wasn't a threat to him.

Brain Shortcuts

Does the smell of a hot dog make you think of attending your first major-league baseball game? Or does a chocolatey s'more remind you of summer camp?

It's not just negative memories that get assigned emotional tags. Memories of all experiences form neural pathways that link those events with meaning and emotional associations, creating mental shortcuts for quicker processing in the future. When we encounter similar sensory cues, they often trigger reminders of the last time we felt that way—sometimes without us even realizing it.

Imagine the hundreds of thousands of neural pathways wired together by experiences of people, places, and situations, each containing sensory triggers of positive and negative emotions associated with needs, outcomes, and resulting beliefs. We'll get into this more in Chapter 12, but both good and bad experiences create associations that cause us to predict outcomes. Our first experiences of a thing lay the foundation for all other experiences, and as these pathways are reinforced, so are the feelings, thoughts, behaviors, and beliefs about whether our needs *will be* met or not, and how that means we need to act. From our early attachment experiences, we begin to form core beliefs such as: "I am seen, known, loved, and important to others and my needs can get met," or conversely, "I am not and it's hopeless," or "I need to do [X] to get my need met." These beliefs fuel emotions and shape our thoughts in everyday interactions, often operating on an unconscious or subconscious level. As a result, powerful emotions and reactions can arise without us fully understanding why. Until we investigate our automatic thoughts, feelings, and behaviors shaped by these brain shortcuts, we'll continue to subconsciously anticipate similar outcomes and act in familiar patterns, unknowingly reinforcing the very experiences we hope to avoid.

> Beliefs fuel emotions and shape our thoughts in everyday interactions, often operating on an unconscious or subconscious level.

When Oliver heard the dog barking, he was immediately and subconsciously taken back to his grandmother's backyard, reacting in much the same way. The amygdala does not perceive time; that concept is not held in this part of the brain. This is why dangerous experiences can feel like they last for an eternity, even though they are only a few seconds. The amygdala doesn't reason about the differences between now and when you may have been smaller and less capable. It's like a movie from that earlier moment was paused, and when triggered, suddenly resumes playing again. Paused movies pick back up in exactly the same spot, regardless of how much time has passed in real life. Similarly, with the amygdala, the threatening experience gets frozen in time, and then associations to that stimulus can pull you right back to the same emotions and reactions you had in the original moment. And because language originates from the PFC, we can lose access to words during stressful events.

Insecure Attachment Styles React, Rather Than Respond

No one chooses their attachment style. It is simply a process our brains have learned to anticipate needs and keep us safe. And just as fight, flight, and freeze are the different adaptive reactions to perceived threats, they also tend to correspond with the predominant reaction in each insecure attachment style. Vacillators most often fight or pursue because they learned to "protest" to get their inconsistent parent's attention. Controllers typically default to fight as well, since freeze and flight often kept them in danger. Avoiders tend to choose flight first, distancing themselves from uncomfortable interactions, and may shift to fight second if they can't escape. Meanwhile Pleasers and Victims are more likely to freeze, feeling stuck or powerless in the face of conflict.

Here are some examples of what these reactions look like in relationships.

Fight—Pursuing to Get Noticed

Jared is not afraid of confrontation. He pursues with complaints and criticisms, and when that doesn't work, he protests by doing something hurtful to get his wife Emma's attention. He wants Emma to feel the hurt he does. He reasons, "If she could feel how she hurt me, she would understand my pain."

Flight—Withdrawing to Protect

When Jared has his outbursts, Emma distances and busies herself in the office while he watches TV. She's tired of his outbursts, so she stays away waiting for him to get over it.

Freeze or Fawn—"Freezing or Pleasing"

Richard's wife, Evelyn, sulks when she feels disappointed in him. Richard scurries around trying to think of anything he can to try and appease her so she won't be mad at him anymore. While Oliver's reaction with Pickles was a classic freeze, Richard's reaction is a type of freeze known as fawning, by which a person reacts to perceived threats by complying or doing what they think the other person wants, to make the danger subside.

While we may interchange the words "responding" and "reacting" at times, they are not the same. When your doctor says you *responded* to a medication, that's good. If she says you *reacted* to it, that's bad. This is the reason we call the emergency services First Responders and not First Reactors! They respond to danger by running toward it when everyone else is reacting and running away from it. Emergency responders create lifelike scenarios and run mock drills to teach their amygdala that the PFC should maintain control in an emergency so they know what to do in different types of situations. When you can accurately assess the situation and choose the most appropriate action based on the circumstance, *you learn to respond*, revising your initial automatic impulse reaction.

Revising Your Experience

Knowing how to be aware when the amygdala hijack is coming on, how to slow it down, and how to reengage the PFC is the key process to facilitating your growth. What is essential, though, is a new experience in which that new conscious awareness can take root. You cannot reason your way out of something you have experienced your way into. Therefore, forming new positive associations to combat your triggers is the only way to reduce your reactions to them.

Imagine if I decided to go skydiving. I would make a conscious decision using my PFC to first learn in a safe environment how to put on a parachute, pull the cord, and land properly when I reach the ground. Yet my instinctive fear of heights may kick in once I'm standing in the doorway looking

> You cannot reason your way out of something you have experienced your way into.

three thousand feet down. My amygdala will tell me this is a bad idea. I might freeze, or want to run away, saying, "I changed my mind." I might even need a push. My PFC and my amygdala will wrestle with the experience all the way down. But if I land safely and the experience is enjoyable, I can manage to form an association of jumping with conquering fear. The next time I go I may not need a push. My PFC may still wrestle with my amygdala, but I now have gained an experience to know I can be okay. And each time I go it will get easier.

I don't think professional skydivers are in the habit of pushing people out, by the way. Are they? I guess I'll find out if I ever go skydiving!

We must first learn not to react before we can learn to respond. We overcome our amygdala hijacks in relational threats by making the subconscious conscious, and bringing these automatic processes into our awareness with our PFC. I think most people understand that a trigger is something that sets us off to react, but *what* is being triggered, and *why*? Reminders of significant emotional wounds cue our reptilian brain to activate automatic "survival shortcuts." But once we're aware of the effect amygdala hijacking has on us and that an old movie is replaying, we can identify our triggers and the subconscious automatic thoughts, feelings, and behaviors we repeat. This creates the conditions for these reactions to move from our subconscious to our conscious, and we can learn to replace them with adaptive, chosen responses.

The Observing Self

To notice our triggers and reactivity we must develop a part of our self-awareness called the "observing self." The term was coined by Dr. Steven Hayes, who developed "Acceptance and Commitment Therapy."[*] The observing self is more than just watching. It's the part of us

---

[*] Steven C. Hayes, Kirk D. Strosahl, and Kelly G. Wilson, *Acceptance and Commitment Therapy: An Experimental Approach to Behavior Change* (Guilford Press, 2004).

that notices and considers actively. When we watch television, it's passive. A science experiment, on the other hand, involves observation, documenting **what you noticed happened when two elements came together—the reaction—and then considering a hypothesis as to why.**

The way to develop your observing self is to notice emotional reactivity, and ask:

1. What am I *feeling*?
2. What's *happening* around me right now, or what just happened?
3. How am I *reacting* to get the corresponding need met or to manage my need not getting met?
4. When in my history did I have similar associations and *learn* that reaction?

By simply observing, we can become aware of our triggers and when they took root.

Consider Judy's story. At the start of a session, Judy announced, "I want to know why I seem to do most of the work in my friendships, and then, when others aren't reciprocating, I can't seem to let the friendship go, even though I know it is clearly declining."

It was a great question. I'd known Judy was having challenges with some friends and feeling like she was on the outside of the circle. From previous sessions, I also knew some of her childhood history. After asking Judy to tell me about a few of her past and current declining friendships, I said, "Judy, I know you felt like you had to earn your mother's approval, which seemed to come so easily for your sister. That training probably makes it pretty familiar to be in the role of putting in the greater effort."

"True. But I know my mother loved me and wouldn't give up on me. She just connected with me in different ways than with my sister who was more like her." She paused a moment considering how to clarify. "I just feel so scared letting friendships go, even though I know I can't save them."

Her mention of being "scared" sounded like fear of abandonment and sudden loss. "Judy, did you ever have a sudden loss of a friend or one move away in childhood?" I asked, taking a guess.

Judy sat silent for a few moments reflecting. "Oh my gosh, that was decades ago, but when I was in high school, my best friend was diagnosed with cancer. She slowly declined over the following eight months and died in the summer before my junior year." Judy began to tear up and I handed her a tissue. "We were like sisters. Her last two months were the worst. I snuck her out one night to go to the drive-in, but we had to come back early because she was so sick. Time was ticking by, and I just wanted one more good memory with her. I cried all night the day she died, and I went through the remainder of high school without a best friend.

"I felt something similar in my twenties when a good friend moved to the other side of the country. We tried to stay in touch, but our lives just went in different directions. Back then there wasn't texting and social media to keep you connected. Wow, I've never made that connection before."

Judy's feelings now made a lot more sense to her. Watching her best friend slip away as a teen, and then as a young adult, having her best friend move, she feels a similar grief when she's not able to keep connections now.

After that session Judy had a story to put to her feelings, helping her build her coherent narrative. Now whenever those feelings resurface for Judy, she can know where they came from and use her PFC to manage those feelings. As she learns to soothe, instead of continuing to *react* by putting in more effort than others, she will be able to *respond* to the changes in relationships, knowing whatever happens, she will be okay.

Over the years I've witnessed many experiences of people making powerful and significant links like this. With a bit of practice putting on the observing self, most are able to make these associations themselves. Judy's underlying feelings were fear of abandonment and loss. But being able to consider when she felt those strong feelings before, and with my observation over what it sounded like she was reacting to, she made the connection.

Once explained, these links can seem obvious. But it's continually surprising how many people don't initially see them because they are simply on the outside of their conscious awareness. Like trying to find something in the dark: The thing you are looking for could be right in front of you, but you can't see. You need someone to shed some light on it for it to become visible. As you cultivate your observing self, insights will become possible, and your coherent narrative can begin to develop.

Using Hindsight for Insight

Self-awareness comes from *hindsight* to see how the past shaped us, *insight* to see how it's affecting our present, and *foresight* to anticipate how we'll be affected in the future *unless we make a change.*

While self-awareness involves developing the "observing self," you will at times need feedback from others too. Someone may observe, "You're so quiet. Do you feel anxious?" or "You're great with kids. Have you thought about working with them?" Sometimes people are way off, and sometimes they're not. We all have blind spots and can use the help of an outside observer, like I did with Judy. Having trusted, impartial people in your life you give permission to share their feedback with you helps you create a fuller picture of yourself.

The more you practice observing yourself, the more you reinforce it, allowing you to keep it turned on longer. When you can observe and learn to manage triggers and reactivity in a present situation, this provides the new experience you need to create a diversion from the old neural pathway.

You can't effectively practice this work without developing your observing self, but also you can't grow without others you can trust. After all, secure attachment doesn't happen if you have no one to attach to!

And to Judy's valid desire, it's all the better to have others who have known you and cared for a long time. The more of these wonderful folks you can find, the more hindsight you'll have available from your life for future insight.

Next, let's dig deeper into this observing practice to look for the two main barriers to greater emotional intelligence.

REFLECT

1. What significant negative experiences have you had and how have these affected the way you react?

2. What associations have you formed to strong feelings such as abandonment, fear, and inadequacy as a result of these experiences?

3. Are you aware when your amygdala is hijacking your brain?

4. Do you most often fight, flight, freeze, or fawn?

5. Can you think of what you have intentionally done to develop your "observing self"?

Chapter Four

Knowing Thyself

I'm so sorry, Kevin! My phone died and there was an accident on the freeway that backed up the traffic. Please don't be mad!'"

Kevin was telling me a story of some progress he had made between the sessions. His girlfriend had arrived late for their date, and in previous situations this had triggered Kevin's emotional abandonment wounds.

"Kelly thought I'd be upset, and usually I would have been, but I've been working on noticing where I carry the stress in my body. I took some deep breaths, like you showed me, and tried to gather myself before she showed up," Kevin shared. "It was tight right here in my chest, but this time I told myself, 'Sometimes, people are late, and I'm going to be okay.'"

He went on to explain that when he noticed he'd started feeling emotionally reactive, he knew he wasn't feeling *mad* as much as *anxious* and *sad*. "It made me think of what we talked about last session, of when I was a kid, and my dad lived out of state. I told Kelly about that and how a few times when he was supposed to visit, he just didn't show up. And this felt a lot like that."

"Wow, great insight and response!" I said, nodding with approval. "And how did Kelly respond?"

"She hugged my arm and told me not to feel sad because she was here now."

"And did you stop feeling sad when she said that?" I asked, suspecting what his answer would be.

"Not quite, but I knew she meant well." I smiled, and we moved on.

Why Emotional Intelligence Matters

I'm eager to get to describing the attachment styles in the next section. But before we do, we need to look at barriers to emotional intelligence that stop us from building our observing self. For if you can't accurately identify your emotions, you might not be able to identify your true needs or have accurate information to make associations to your past. Kevin's ability to recognize, understand, and manage his physical symptoms and anger helped him see it was anxiety and sadness that were most affecting his thinking and behavior. It's because he was able to tap into these emotions that he made the connection to his historical wound. That is true emotional intelligence.

Another reason emotional intelligence matters is that understanding our own mind and emotions is fundamental to understanding another's. Developing this self-awareness enables empathy—recognizing how emotions impact others—to know how to respond to emotional needs. And responding to emotional needs is the opportunity to build connection behind every relational interaction.

> Understanding our own mind and emotions is fundamental to understanding another's.

When you experience something firsthand, you gain an inside understanding of it. Some insecurely attached people struggle to experience empathy because anxiety pushes their *true* emotions down, burying them under fear, anger, or shame. And this blinds them to the inside information about themselves that could help them join with what others are feeling in a given moment.

What Kelly showed Kevin was sympathy. Sympathy acknowledges another person's emotional state and is an emotion in itself, which you feel *toward* another person. However, sympathy is not necessarily feeling the same emotion the other person is feeling. I can feel sorry for someone who misses their flight, though they might be feeling more anxious about what their boss might say when they can't be at work the next day. **Empathy, though, is not a feeling in itself, but a social-emotional cognitive process where we share in the same emotion *with* the other person**, even if it that's not with the same intensity. While Kelly didn't do anything wrong and tried the best she could to connect with Kevin in that moment, she didn't *share* the same emotion because she tried to quickly move him out of it.

Empathy cannot coexist with the urge to change someone's emotion. Pleasers, as we'll soon see, often try to shift others' feelings to alleviate their own discomfort. Feeling anxious themselves over others' distress, they try to cheer others up to ease their own anxiety. While it might seem like it's done for the other's benefit, this is ultimately self-protective, and self-serving.

So many times, the wounds we subconsciously carry are projected on others and it prevents us from seeing where our past is impacting our present. You will need to learn to see these to gain insight and motivation to grow from your insecure attachment style. The point of growth occurs only when the pain of feeling insecure exceeds the pain that you perceive others to be doing to you. That's when you can decide to take care of your insecurities once and for all.

Socrates famously said, "Know thyself," emphasizing self-awareness as an important path to true wisdom. Without understanding your own emotions, triggers, and reactions, it's impossible to understand another's. Not too long ago, I had a phone call with a wife inquiring about couples therapy. She told me she and her husband were struggling because he did not seem to know how to connect with her in her emotions. "I feel sad for him," she said, "because I know he wants us to have a good marriage. Deep down he must be feeling sad too because he doesn't know how." I was surprised at her level of insight and empathy for her husband, because the feeling I most often hear expressed when people call me for couples therapy is "frustration" at the other person. She told me she had done some individual growth work already, and I suspect she is going to progress well because she has developed a strong empathetic function.

What Drives Our Anger?

Not too long ago, Kevin would have responded differently too, likely answering his girlfriend's apology with annoyance at her for not keeping her phone charged or not leaving earlier. Anger is a secondary emotion, meaning it arises as a result of another feeling. Anger acts as a bodyguard for more vulnerable emotions we subconsciously believe we can't safely express because we believe the need won't be met or understood. Anger most often protects hurt, fear, or shame.

If you trip and your friend laughs at you, you might get cross at him, but beneath that is the sting of embarrassment. If your teenager turns off her phone and stays out beyond her curfew, you might be angry when she returns home, but that stems from the worry you felt at not knowing where she was or what may have happened to her. And if a group of friends go out without inviting you, you may get mad, but that anger results from feeling rejected. The protective shield of anger doesn't just stop us from sharing our vulnerable emotions, it also stops others from connecting with those emotions. Unless the underlying core emotional wound is acknowledged and addressed, the corresponding need behind it remains unmet, and your anger will remain.

So, is anger ever adaptive? Yes, anger is a necessary and healthy emotion when we need *to protect ourselves or others from real emotional or physical harm*. For example, if someone physically attacks you or your family, that surge of anger provides the adrenaline boost needed to act and quickly defend. Likewise, anger can be a powerful motivator when we witness injustice, spurring us into action to advocate for those who are marginalized or mistreated. However, *anger becomes maladaptive when used to harm ourselves or others*, especially when it's a strategy to get attention or assert control.

Though many people express anger at a lack of attention, closeness, or connection because they desire this, anger often has the opposite effect, pushing others away and keeping us separated. Feelings like "frustration," "annoyance," and "irritation" are all just different variations of anger reflecting the levels of intensity on the anger spectrum. If it feels safer to get angry and push others away it's likely because you did not receive comfort or validation for your emotional pain growing up. Learning to look beneath anger requires a high level of emotional intelligence.

> Learning to look beneath anger requires a high level of emotional intelligence.

If It's Hysterical, It's Historical!

When Kevin noticed his feelings felt bigger than what should be natural for someone waiting on another person who's just a few minutes late, he realized there was a core emotional wound from his past. Fortunately, he was understanding more about how his past continues to affect him and he'd decided he no longer wanted to reinforce the habit of picking up that defensive shield. Anger is just one self-protective coping strategy people employ. Other common self-protective reactions to hurt are

- minimizing, denying, avoiding, or running away so you don't have to acknowledge the problem;
- blaming others or defending actions so you don't have to look at your flaws;
- fixing, appeasing, or pleasing to make the problem go away; and
- protesting (criticizing, sulking, pouting, stonewalling, detaching) so others notice your pain without having to share vulnerably and ask for your needs.

All of these are contained in the five insecure attachment styles we'll discuss coming up. Now, I'm not saying some of these things can't be adaptive. Avoiding a bully or mean person is often the best thing to do. Detaching emotionally from someone after a breakup is necessary. As is distracting yourself for small periods during times of overwhelming physical or emotional pain after an injury or loss that you know will take time to heal. But when these become default reflexive *reactions* rather than adaptive *responses*, and are used as shields rather than to grow or build relationships, this is where they become maladaptive. Reactions are repeated actions—a *re-action*. This word derives from the Latin "reactio." The prefix "re" means "back" or "again" and "actio" is a verb meaning "to act." So, "reactio" means "to do again" or "to act back." Therefore, to react is to act back from our past.

Carl Jung, the Swiss psychiatrist known for his work on the unconscious in dreams and memories, wrote, "When an inner situation is not made conscious, it happens outside, as fate. That is to say, when the individual remains undivided and does not become conscious of his inner opposite, the world must perforce act out the conflict and be torn into opposing halves."* In other words, we unconsciously (or subconsciously) create a false sense of self on the inside that we act out in the world. For ease of remembering, Jung's insight is often paraphrased as: "Until you make the unconscious conscious, it will direct your life, and you will call it fate." It's a phrase I often reflect on and one I encourage you to also remember.

Difficult situations and strong emotions can bring out maladaptive reactions, or they can be a launch pad for growth. Recognizing our self-protective strategies and understanding their origins—while taking ownership of our emotions—releases others from the responsibility to manage *our* unhealed wounds. By bringing our self-protective strategies

---

* C. G. Jung, *Aion: Researches into the Phenomenology of the Self* (Princeton University Press, 1959).

into conscious awareness, we engage our PFC, allowing capability to override the reactive amygdala that is falsely interpreting a present situation as a threat based on our past experiences.

Another paraphrase of Jung's work is: "Everything that irritates us about others can lead us to an understanding of ourselves." And this deeper understanding of ourselves can help shape our coherent narrative (understanding our story), so we can move beyond anger and frustration, and instead recognize opportunities to manage our reactivity and build more secure connections with others.

You need to first stop reacting, before you can start responding. Only then can you lower the shield and be open to have the new experience needed to create new neural pathways. You'll find **growth goals** for how to do this in the following chapters.

> You need to first stop reacting, before you can start responding.

How Hidden Shame Overpowers

One last thing before we get to the attachment styles. Because shame is such a major barrier to growth, and prevalent in all the attachment styles, we need to deal with it specifically. Remember Erickson's second stage of development (from Chapter 2)? When a child does not learn to trust in his or her abilities because normative exploration is prevented or not approved of, he or she personalizes this experience and comes to believe they are not lovable in some way. A parent's voice often becomes their child's inner monologue. In therapy, I sometimes point this out when I hear someone speak harshly about themselves. I'll ask, "Whose voice is that—yours or a parent's?" Almost always they recognize it's a parent's voice they've internalized. That realization can be a powerful first step toward rewriting that inner script of shame.

While guilt and shame are similar emotions, with guilt, our focus is on our action, regarding that as the mistake or the thing that was wrong or bad. Because actions can be changed, guilt can serve a helpful purpose to lead us to reflect, repent, and choose a different path going forward. But with shame, our focus is on our sense of self, where we believe we are the mistake—flawed and defective. The internal message of guilt is "I did something wrong," whereas the internal message of shame is "There's something wrong with me!" It's harder to change our personhood than it is an action. Shame makes us feel unworthy of love, belonging, and connection, and it manifests in negative labels we assign to ourselves—"bad," "worthless," "unlovable," or "stupid." Shame is often accompanied by feeling powerless and disconnected, causing us to dwell on mistakes and making us want to hide.

We develop shame not because we experience difficult emotions, but because our first experiences of difficult emotions did not involve acceptance, comfort, reassurance, or protection when we needed it. Making mistakes, getting things wrong, feeling fear or embarrassment, and experiencing physical pain are normal experiences for everyone, especially children. An attuned attachment figure helps a child process these things. Acceptance, comfort, reassurance, and protection are the emotional needs to reduce shame by showing us we're still loved, and therefore intrinsically worthy of connection. However, when a child is dismissed or ridiculed for having these experiences, they develop beliefs of unworthiness.

We all experience shame at times. The most common form of shame is transient shame which is brief and situational and experienced after a public mistake or being caught when our actions don't align with our values. It's uncomfortable, but usually short-lived and easier to recognize. Other than transient shame, I used to believe living with shame meant a person had low self-esteem and was fearful to try new things or make new friends because they anticipated failure at every turn. This is called chronic shame. I reasoned that I was a confident person, so therefore I didn't struggle with shame. Sure, I had some regrets that, if I thought about it, I felt some brief shame over, but when I wasn't thinking about those things, I was fine. Having this mindset kept me from seeing the role secret shame played in my life.

Secret shame is the experience of feeling shame about feeling shame. It's a hidden, often unconscious form of shame that can be deeply damaging. We tuck it away—sometimes so well that even we aren't fully aware of it. When secret shame operates below the surface, it works covertly, shaping how we relate to ourselves and others. People who carry secret shame struggle to admit mistakes or acknowledge their flaws. They may use anger or defensiveness to protect themselves from being "found out," and blame others when they feel bad trying to "prove" they're not unworthy or unlovable.

Chris struggles with secret shame. He can't stop thinking about his penalty miss last night at the game. His soccer team was down 0–1, and he had the chance to level the score. He wants to impress his teammates because he is new on the team. He hadn't stepped up to take the penalty, but his teammates had encouraged him to go for it. Now what do they think of him since this miss cost the game? He had a hard time falling asleep that night, and the penalty miss continues to bother him the next day. He resolves to try even harder the next game because he needs his teammates to know he is good enough to play alongside them.

Chris doesn't realize it, but secret shame is driving his dwelling on negative feelings about the game. He's a confident person in many other ways, which has made him successful at work. If you asked him, he wouldn't identify that he struggles with shame. He thinks shame makes a person too fearful to try, and he is determined to try even harder now. Chris's shame is manifesting in his insecurity that his new teammates won't think he is good enough and his fear that they may not ask him to come back next season. This is rooted in his past. Chris didn't make the soccer team in college. His best friend, Greg, did. They had played together on a successful high school soccer team. He and Greg picked the same college with plans to have an amazing adventure together. However, he and Greg drifted apart as Greg grew closer to his new soccer teammates and Chris felt rejected. Now his fears of potential rejection are manifesting with this new team.

For some people, just acknowledging their feelings and reactivity brings shame, so they justify their behavior as the way they inherently are rather than how they've been shaped.

Consider Morgan. She has a hard exterior shell she presents to others and describes herself as a tomboy having grown up with three older brothers. She's married to Patrick. Both are highly independent, which works for most of their daily life, up until when Morgan has to admit she does have needs that Patrick's not meeting. Patrick was trying his best to learn the skills in therapy. When I tried to take them through the Comfort Circle to talk through a disagreement, Morgan resisted. Her way of sharing her feelings was to tell Patrick, "If you would stop being an [expletive], and get your [expletive] together, then we wouldn't keep having this problem!" When I tried to redirect Morgan to use more vulnerable words to engage Patrick and encourage him to feel some empathy for her, she exclaimed angrily, "This emotional fluff is BS! It's not how I talk."

Morgan wasn't allowed to show her emotions growing up. Her mom had died when she was young, and her single-parent dad didn't know how to deal with her feelings. He sent her to her room whenever she cried until she "got over it." Morgan learned to "get over it" quickly, since crying meant rejection and isolation. She was now modeling the same lack of empathy to Patrick that her father showed her. She described herself as "not a hugger," which made it difficult for her to receive comfort from Patrick to soothe the strong anger that was covering the shame inside of her. Morgan's dad shamed her for feeling fear, hurt, and sadness, and now these emotions were unacceptable for her or anyone else to have. They meant she was "bad," which created a pathway of shame. The emotions we don't allow ourselves to feel often become the very ones that make us uncomfortable, or even irritated, when we see them expressed by others. Morgan believed this was who she was and there was no changing her, so Patrick needed to adapt.

When we believe we have no choice other than to remain the way we currently are, then the only solution we see is for others to simply accept our traits and adjust to us. This mindset offers a form of protection—we avoid the discomfort of taking responsibility, facing our shame, and pursuing growth. But in doing so, shame quietly holds us back, keeping us stuck and preventing true healing and transformation. *"Who we are"* and *"how we are"* are two different things. There are intrinsic parts of us that can't be changed—like being an introvert or an extrovert. We're just born that way. But *how* we attach is learned and so can be changed.

Disarming Covert Shame

If you experience secret shame, pay attention to how often you compare yourself to others or expect others to adjust for you to feel better. Does this come from a need for acceptance? We overcome shame by first acknowledging and exploring it. We can't work on something we don't admit. Once we can admit shame, we can then ask ourselves, where in my history does this come from? With whom, or what's the earliest situation I can remember feeling this shame? Did a teacher embarrass me in front of a class? Did a parent shame me when I got things wrong or did things they did not like?

Next, we must offer ourselves the love and acceptance we so desire. Several years ago, a former neighbor of mine was selling his house and moving to another state. I casually asked if he'd been preapproved for a mortgage on his next home, and he exclaimed, "I don't need preapproval. I'm self-approved!" He went on to explain that the equity he had in his current house would be more than enough to pay for his next house outright, so he wouldn't need preapproval for a loan. Shame splits us into two. How we feel about ourselves is influenced by how we think people feel toward us. When we can accept our flaws as areas to grow in, we can be *self-approved*, no longer bound to what others may think of us, and independent of them needing to make adjustment for us to feel better. When we can acknowledge actions as mistakes, they no longer define our worth.

I don't mean to imply it's possible to be completely "shame-free," or that shame is always a "bad" emotion (no emotions are good or bad in and of themselves). Shame tells us where we've been wounded by others, which we all have, or how we've gone against our values. Living in shame though is not good because it keeps us isolated and lonely. But, if we can make sense of it, it reveals an emotional need for our healing.

Finally, we remove shame's power with confession. Shame only thrives in an environment of silence and isolation. Confession takes away the power of shame because a shame reaction causes us to want to run away. But when we admit we feel shame and bring the flaw or wound causing it into light, we face it head on and it loses its power over us. Taking accountability for our mistakes causes cognitive dissonance (an uneasy feeling of a discrepancy between our values and our actions), which is the catalyst for growth. We resolve the discrepancy by either changing the way we think or changing how we act.

> Shame only thrives in an environment of silence and isolation.

Here's Harper's story. She's a self-published children's book author and illustrator who came to a session in tears over a printing mistake in her latest book. She was so upset at herself for not catching it and now it was mass printed. Since Harper's books bring awareness to mental health challenges for children, I suggested, instead of hoping people didn't notice, doing the opposite and publicly admitting the mistake on her social media accounts. She could use it to show mistakes happen, and that self-acceptance connects us through vulnerability. She loved the idea, and her base of customers connected with it too because it was the vulnerable message kids need to hear: Adults make mistakes too and mistakes can be recoverable. Harper sold out of all the misprinted books in a matter of days!

Okay, I think you're finally ready now to look at the attachment styles, so let's get to it after you consider these questions.

REFLECT

1. How emotionally intelligent do you consider yourself? Are you able to regularly identify a range of emotions you experience and connect them to corresponding needs?

2. Are you aware of and can you communicate vulnerable primary emotions under your anger?

3. How many of these self-protective strategies sounded familiar for what you regularly do?

4. Have you been struggling with secret shame that you've not been aware of?

5. Did you have a parent who helped you process challenges, mistakes, and difficult emotions with acceptance, empathy, comfort, and reassurance?

6. Can you differentiate between "who you are" and "how you are"? How eager do you feel to learn more skills to address your current shortcomings?

Step Two

Become More Aware

> Your vision will become clear only when you can look into your own heart.... Who looks outside, dreams; who looks inside, awakes.
>
> Carl Jung

Having a learned insecure attachment style does not necessarily mean we are "insecure" in the sense that we are unsure of ourselves as an individual. Rather, the bond formed in childhood to our primary caregiver(s) was an insecure one, in that we did not build trust they could, or would, be available to consistently attune to our physical and emotional needs and comfort us. The responsibility for providing what is needed to build a secure attachment lies with the caregiver, not the child. Therefore, the formation of secure attachment depends on the caregiver's ability and availability to meet the child's needs. Forming an insecure attachment is *not* our fault, and sometimes, not even the adult's—it could simply have been unawareness or inability to give what was needed.

A reminder here again, this is not about blaming parents; it's about explaining the why and how. Sometimes, life situations affect the cycle of bonding, such as premature births or postpartum depression. This does not mean caregivers were uncaring, or unloving, or that none of the child's needs were met. Most of the time, it means caregivers lacked awareness of how to meet a child's deeper emotional needs for the child to feel secure in that bond, or the caregiver struggled to control their own emotions and reactivity due to their own learned insecure attachment style.

Many of us grew up with two parents who we formed independent relationships with and learned to bond to each in different ways. What was accepted or tolerated with one may not have been with the other. Others grew up with three or more caregivers, depending on whether your biological parents separated and remarried, or how involved grandparents or other family members were in your childhood. You may also have had key influential people in your life, such as coaches, teachers, or pastors who took a vested interest in your development and so became attachment figures for periods during your childhood. There are even some individuals who had radically different periods in their childhoods depending on the choices their parents made, such as being with a dangerous partner for a few years and then with a loving one. Or a parent went into or came out of addiction for part of your childhood, and their responsiveness or availability changed during these times. Maybe you spent time in foster care and had varying experiences in the different homes with those who cared for you.

It's possible for a child to form more secure bonds with some attachment figures than others. Of course, the caregivers we spend the most time with, and the ones who have the most responsibility to meet our needs, have the most significant impact. Each of our attachment relationships has shaped the ways we bond with others.

Attachment injuries can be seen on a spectrum from mild to severe depending on how well our caregivers controlled their own reactivity, understood their own feelings and emotional needs, and helped us understand, express, and verbalize ours. Our attachment styles developed from how we learned to get our needs met (or deal with our needs going unmet). These coping strategies, which have now become ways of reacting and which shaped our attachment, were developed because they served a purpose in childhood. They were adaptive at the time, and with the caregiver we developed them with, even if they were nonadaptive with others. It's now, in adulthood, that these dysfunctions do not serve us as we have more power and greater responsibility for ourselves and to others, to provide for their needs and get our needs met in relationships. This is true even in the relationships we have with our parents now as an adult.

Most people have a primary attachment style, but don't get hung up if some of the descriptions of your predominant type don't feel true for you. As you open yourself to feedback and cultivate your observing self, your insecurities will become clearer, and you might become aware of the things you initially dismissed as you grow. You may also have a blend of two or more styles from the strategies you had to use at different times or with different people growing up. The goal here is to develop the observing self and understand why you get triggered, how you react, and what are better strategies to develop so you can improve your relationships. Secure attachment is the goal.

> No one will ever be totally free from any type of insecurity. The good news is, we can all continually grow.

You may have already done some growth work in adulthood and find some of these things were true for you before but no longer are. If you do have, or when you finally feel like you've earned, secure attachment, that might just mean you're more secure than insecure. However, being 51 percent of the way somewhere still leaves a long way to go! Also, no one has a perfect childhood, and so we all have some insecurities we've developed maladaptive strategies for. No one will ever be totally free from any type of insecurity. The good news is, we can all continually grow in the areas we're deficient in, once we know better and take a realistic view of ourselves and how we've been shaped. This is exactly what building a coherent narrative is about!

As you read through each description, I suggest highlighting what's true for you and returning to it again to check your progress as you grow. You may even benefit from asking your parents about your childhood and what type of child you were and their memories of you. Doing this, you may find more about how your early childhood shaped you, even if you don't have a narrative memory of it. This can help you make sense of implicit (emotional and bodily feeling) memories you may have.

Remember, attachment, whether secure or insecure, is programming. And what was programmed can be *reprogrammed*.

Chapter Five

Avoiders Feel "Fine"

Thirty-year-old Lauren noticed how safe and secure her young children felt with her husband. He took time to ask about their feelings when they were hurt or scared, while she found herself uncomfortable when her kids showed emotions. During conversations in therapy, she also noticed how her discomfort with emotions impacted her relationship with her husband—she found herself feeling stifled when he wanted to get close to her. Calling her mother one night after my suggestion, Lauren hesitantly brought this all up with her.

"Mom, I think I'm still affected by that time when I saw dad hitting you."

"What? You were only three, Lauren. You can't possibly remember what happened accurately. Your dad struggled with alcohol for a year and then he quit, and everything has been fine since. Therapists always want to try and blame people's problems on a past 'trauma,'" her mom said sarcastically. "What your dad did had nothing to do with me, and it has nothing to do with you."

And that was that. Lauren's mother responded exactly as she'd been raised by her own parents to respond—dismissively.

Childhood Experience and Relationship with Parents

The Avoider attachment style can form from a variety of parenting approaches that include

- strict or rigid parenting that prioritizes behavioral compliance through consequences over relationship-building;
- a focus on the child needing to maintain parental-set standards for household tasks or chores;
- limited physical affection or discussion of emotions initiated by the parent;
- an over-focus on the child's ability to achieve in the area the parent deems important—academics, athletics, or the arts;
- a lack of one-on-one time spent with the child; and
- limited care (which may have happened because of a single-parent home), forcing the child to take responsibility for their own needs too early on.

Parents may have been physically available, present at events, consistent in providing for physical needs, but not very emotionally responsive, especially when the child really needed comfort. Avoiders were encouraged to be, or out of necessity became, independent early on in life and didn't receive much affection, tenderness, or discussion of emotions. The focus was on self-reliance or responsibility-building, and performing to get the parent's approval or gain privileges. Avoider parents often value mastery of skills and discourage the expression of feelings or needs. This can be overtly communicated by telling the child, "You're fine," or through unspoken messages the child picks up on that the parent is uncomfortable with affection. If they had an Avoider parent, Avoiders often report they rarely or never heard parents say "I love you" during their childhood.

Because no one is available to help them make sense of their feelings, the child forming an Avoider attachment style manages their emotions by dismissing them and restricting their needs. They pick up on an underlying message that their parents don't want to get to know them on a deep level, and by accomplishing tasks, not making a fuss, or not showing their emotions, they learn to suppress their needs (physical or emotional) and take care of themselves.

> **The child forming an Avoider attachment style manages their emotions by dismissing them and restricting their needs.**

Common Views of the World and Relationships

Most Avoiders describe their childhoods as typical and might say that as a child, "I knew my parents loved me," and give examples of being provided for or parents being present at their games and events. But when asked about memories of their parents demonstrating tender love or comfort, they struggle to find specific examples. Avoiders tend not to think about negative attachment events because they learned to suppress these memories along with their emotions. So, they recall their childhood as mainly positive.

Adult Avoiders, like Lauren's mother, want others to deal with negative emotions in the way they do—by dismissing and restricting them. They tend to have a reduced capacity for empathy, not because they're uncaring, but because they don't know what unrestricted emotions feel like in order to connect with the other person's pain. Validating emotions for others requires acknowledging it makes sense to feel them. Since Avoiders live in relative emotional neutrality, they don't understand why others allow themselves to feel negative emotion. They often think others who feel deeply are "too emotional," or "too sensitive," which they see as weakness that reduces resiliency. Independence and responsibility are the Avoider's highest values, since these were the main lessons they learned in childhood. They see asking for help as weakness.

Avoiders place a strong emphasis on their performance because they were trained to be independent at a young age. This often helps them in their careers. Western culture can praise independence, resilience, stoicism, and "get-it-done" attitudes, so lack of emotion is often reinforced in high-performance environments such as school, sports, and work. Avoiders often don't see their lack of emotion as a problem, and some even praise their parent's rigid approach, as the hyper-independence they learned is helping them succeed. The Avoider's stability, consistency, and responsibility are often attractive to others who did not get this from a parent.

Common Internal Feelings

The Avoider attachment is characterized by suppression, dismissal, and avoidance of emotions, so they don't allow themselves to feel much. They tend to believe if you don't have expectations for your needs to be met, you can't be hurt or disappointed. Their solution is to not have needs as much as possible, and because feelings indicate needs, not having needs can only be done by suppressing feelings.

Avoiders who had an emotionally cold parent become empty in their emotional capacity. Emptiness is different from loneliness. Loneliness would mean having experienced emotional closeness and then losing it. This evokes sadness. Emptiness comes from being deprived of emotional closeness. This evokes anger. That's why the negative emotions Avoiders do feel, or are comfortable expressing, are usually stress-related or anger-inducing (frustration, irritation, agitation, annoyance). Anger is not vulnerable and is more acceptable for Western-culture males to feel. Female Avoiders in Western culture, though, are more apt to be labeled as emotionally cold, especially if they are in positions of power or authority.

Avoiders pride themselves on their ability to stay calm on the outside under pressure. They often refer to expressions of negative emotions as a person being "emotional," which means irrational to them and not good. This further devalues the importance of feelings, and they encourage being free of emotion so you can think logically and rationally.

Common Triggers

The Avoider's main triggers are contained in the acronym EVILBUD:

Being pressed for **Emotional Connection**
Vulnerability
Inadequacy
Being **Let down** (or letting others down)
Being **Burdened** (by others' emotions and needs)
Underperforming or being **Unproductive**
Dependency (on or from others)

Avoiders resist emotions mainly because it makes them feel inadequate and this is vulnerable. Their hard work has brought achievement, and because this was the only time they received praise or recognition, when they are criticized, fail, let others down, or underperform, this rattles their core identity. They tend to work harder as the only reasonable resolution to make the feeling of inadequacy go away.

Avoiders are not necessarily people who dislike spending time with others; however, they become uncomfortable when others try to get close or need to rely on them. Emotional connection means being vulnerable, and vulnerability is seen as being "needy." Needing in childhood led to rejection or being let down, so needing anything is interpreted as inadequacy and ultimately weakness. Avoiders could only rely on themselves, and that is what they expect everyone to do. To need is to be dependent, and they don't like to rely on others or others to rely on them. This feels burdensome. Emotional connection is also an area they do not perform well in, so they stay away from being exposed in this area as much as possible.

As Avoiders start to grow and allow themselves to feel and depend on others for their needs, they will notice feelings of shame and anxiety surfacing. Avoiders experience shame from rejection and inadequacy. They initially might think they don't feel rejection, but that's because they've taught themselves not to need others, so they won't experience it. As they learn to not suppress emotions and allow themselves to be vulnerable, they can begin to see their performance standards and dismissal of emotions as avoidant self-protective strategies covering these feelings. Once in recovery and able to admit weakness, Avoiders can add **shame** to their list of triggers and use the acronym EVILBUDS to help develop their observing self.

Common Conflict Patterns with Avoiders

Avoiders run away from conflict, problems, and emotional sharing because they are bothersome to them to deal with. When others share emotions with them, Avoiders often want to fix, problem-solve, or move that person away from their feelings. They're either unsure what others need, don't think it's their responsibility, or they're not comfortable or confident enough to provide for emotional needs. Because they have such a high focus on independence, the Avoider thinks total responsibility to resolve emotions and reactivity should fall on each person, so they should not have to comfort others.

When they do attempt to comfort others it's often with statements like "You'll be okay" or "You don't have to feel that way," or by telling others to just think about their problem more positively. They don't recognize that when you downplay or tell someone to push past their feelings, you are dismissing that person's feelings. They may even try making a joke to get a smile or laugh. These are all things Avoiders do for themselves to move past negative emotions, so it's the only way they know how to help others. Others, though, tend to feel like their pain is not taken seriously or the Avoider doesn't care, and they may get angry, which fuels the conflict cycle and causes the Avoider to dismiss and avoid more. This is a typical dynamic between an Avoider and their spouse.

Many Avoiders have a hard time comprehending the significance of emotional intimacy, so are unaware of what they're missing out on and how important such connection is for others. Because they are so emotionally disconnected, Avoider males struggle with providing the emotional intimacy their wife needs, especially to drive her desire for sexual connection. When connection becomes one-way traffic, spouses get tired of this and may protest to get the Avoider to change. However, Avoiders typically just wait for others to "get over hurt."

Avoiders usually see their style as the most desirable state because they are less "dramatic." They tend not to see their avoidance as fueling negative relationship cycles as much as others who have more outwardly expressed reactivity. They reason that if everyone was as calm and responsible as them, the world would be fine.

> Avoiders typically just wait for others to "get over their hurt."

Reactivity in the Avoider

The evening Lauren spoke to her mother, the call ended quickly. Neither brought it up again.

These are the common Avoider coping strategies for managing stress or conflict:

- Deny, dismiss, or minimize, so they don't have to acknowledge a problem
- Distance or refuse to talk about what is bothering them
- Blame the other person's reactivity as the problem
- Try to fix by offering practical solutions

- Distract self from negative feelings (using work, alcohol, drugs, food, porn, etc.)
- Get angry to prevent others getting too close
- Disconnect and move on, leaving things unresolved

When triggered, the Avoider's primary reaction is to distance and leave the situation. If they have to stay, they will detach and withdraw and will often avoid eye contact. And when they want to escape but can't, they get angry to create space to do so.

Avoiders are often proud of their ability to suppress emotion. They may even receive compliments on how "strong" they appear when going through challenging times, which can reinforce emotional dismissal. Avoidant qualities are also often prized in the corporate world, where it's deemed advantageous for business decisions to not be personal, so company profit and success are prioritized. Unfortunately, we cannot select only negative emotions to repress, so positive emotions (happiness, excitement, and joy) are often muted in Avoiders too. People may find them hard to read and not know exactly how happy or satisfied they are.

Avoiders are masters of compartmentalization, and encourage others to do the same:

- When others are sad, Avoiders say "focus on happy/good things."
- When others are scared, Avoiders say "be brave, there's nothing to be scared of."
- When others are worried or distressed, Avoiders say "it will work out."
- When others are hurt, Avoiders say "tough it out" or "push past the pain."
- When others are angry, Avoiders say "get over it, be logical."

It's usually important to the Avoider for their spouse and children to be resilient like they believe they are. They think resilience is when things don't really bother a person, rather than understanding resilience as a person's ability to appropriately feel their emotions and manage them. They can reason that those who feel emotions are not resilient. They don't recognize there's a difference between resiliency and hardness. Stones are hard, but they chip when dropped. Stress balls are soft, but they can absorb tension and quickly find their shape again.

True resiliency is developed by learning how to feel all of life's emotions and self-soothe. This is learned through the cycle of healthy bonding. Learning not to feel your emotions develops a hardness that prevents others from getting to your soft center, which is where intimacy is developed. To the Avoider though, if family members can be independent, self-sufficient, and not too "emotional," this means that they will be successful in life. Therefore, emotional connection is not really needed from them.

Avoiders may use acts of service as a substitute for telling others they love them or giving physical affection because it's less vulnerable. Avoiders who show love this way usually expect others to reciprocate by completing tasks to demonstrate their love back, though they may get frustrated if others don't complete jobs as well as they do. High-performing Avoiders tend to have low capacity for disorganization, forgetfulness, slowness, or inefficiency from others. They interpret these as "sloppiness," "carelessness," "laziness,' "irresponsibility," or "disrespect" toward them.

When pushed to emotionally connect, Avoiders tend to share thoughts rather than emotions. If you ask them how they are, they're either "good," "fine," or "frustrated." Because vulnerable emotions (worry, fear, overwhelm) make them feel weak, many Avoiders will deny feeling these emotions, even when it is clear they're experiencing them. Putting their reactions down to physical feelings (such as hunger or tiredness) is safer for them to express and makes them feel less inadequate or vulnerable.

Creating Healthy Resolution with the Avoider

Not encouraged to explore their feelings as a child, Avoiders didn't learn much self-reflection. They are used to minimizing, restricting, and dismissing, as this is what they had to do to get through difficult moments in childhood. Having little self-awareness of their own emotions limits awareness of these in others, and they often don't know what to do when someone shares emotions with them.

Avoiders stop dismissing and avoiding when they allow themselves to feel and need. They can only do this by cultivating awareness of their emotions. When you are in the listener role, and the Avoider only gives you facts, ask them to find emotion words so you can understand how the facts impact them. Using a list of emotions as a prompt to consider what they might be feeling will help. (You can get a free list called "Soul Words" at https://howwelove.com/freebies/.) You might suggest what it sounds like to you they are describing feeling, or what you think a person might feel in their situation.

When you are in the speaker role of the Comfort Circle and sharing your feelings, it can help to tell Avoiders that you just need them to listen and empathize, not fix. Above all, try not to take the Avoider's distancing personally. They don't know how to connect emotionally with others. They have learned to soothe by not expecting help, so this is new to them. It's not personal, and they are not holding out on you. They don't yet know the experience of relief that co-regulation with another person provides, so they need gentle and encouraging coaxing to let their guard down to see what that feels like.

If you criticize them, they'll feel inadequate and clam up. Remember, becoming aware, allowing themselves to feel, and putting emotions into words is a new experience for them. As with learning any new skill, this will take time, and you may see a disconnect between stated emotions and facial expressions and tone. They need to unlearn patterns of avoiding, minimizing, restricting, and fixing that have been conditioned into them for decades. As they allow themselves to experience emotions, they will slowly begin to feel them inside their body, and that's when you will see this translate into facial expressions and tone.

Creating word pictures for Avoiders, through telling a story or getting them to visualize and acknowledge how difficult the experiences they went through as a child were, can be impactful. It can be especially powerful to have them imagine what it would be like for one of their own children to have to deal with what they dealt with at the same age. Their only experience has been looking at the world through their eyes from the inside out, so put them on the outside, to help them visualize the vulnerability and limited capacity of a child. This helps them see the responsibility they took on was too much or too early, and that being expected to deal with big feelings by themselves was overwhelming and unfair.

Since Avoiders are used to following a linear pattern, having written directions on how to listen, things to say that sound empathetic, and questions to ask to explore can be helpful. (The Reflect-Connect-Respond technique is a good template for them, or you can download "The Comfort Circle Guide for the Listener" at https://howwelove.com/freebies/.) Giving them scripts for what to ask and say will help them see how to get deeper in conversations. Learning how to use an empathetic tone will take time, as they begin to allow themselves to feel emotions. Showing empathy to them by imagining what it feels like to not be able to recognize emotions can help them find empathy for themselves. If you are recovering from a Vacillator attachment, you may have to tell yourself that your recovering Avoider spouse is practicing, rather than pretending as they learn these skills. Vacillators tend to struggle to accept things that don't feel genuine to them. We'll get more into that later.

Remember, one of the Avoider's triggers is inadequacy, so they will need lots of encouragement in practicing these skills. If you are the spouse of an Avoider, to depersonalize their actions, you will need to find compassion for the little boy or girl they were who did not get comfort and learn about their feelings. This can be hard because they are likely doing to you what their parents did to them. The difference is, this causes you pain since you probably are in touch with your feelings, whereas they learned to turn theirs off, so they don't understand how hurtful their avoidance is to you. It may also be your own childhood emotional injuries that make it more painful for you. Picturing them as a child may help you gather this compassion.

What to Say to Engage the Avoider in Self-Reflection or When They Get Frustrated

Help them link behaviors to emotions:
"*I notice that when (situation X) happens, you get (mention behavior). I wonder if you feel (suggest emotion).*"

Then ask follow-up questions to get them to reflect on how that emotion affects them:
"*Can you share what was going on physically inside you when that happened?*"
"*Help me understand why that is important to you.*"

Validating their emotion and showing understanding models for them how to create connection:
"*It makes sense why you feel that way.*"
"*I can understand why you did that now.*"
"*I would be hurt/worried/sad too if that happened to me.*"

Next, empathize with the emotion:
"That must have been hard for you."
"That sounds like a difficult situation."
"I'm so sorry that happened to you."

Lastly, help them link their feelings to needs. Ask *"What do you need from me right now?"* If they have trouble identifying a need, start with their feeling:
"You said you feel worried, I wonder if you need some reassurance."
"You said you feel sad, I wonder if you need some comfort."
"You said you feel confused, I wonder if you need clarity."

If they try to revert to problem-solving, affirm their need for a solution, but help them see the emotional need as an important part of that solution. Remind them that growth is always uncomfortable, but it will be transformational in the end. By learning to reflect on their inner struggle this will enable them to recognize the same emotions again in the future. And eventually, they'll come to know what they need more quickly and find it's okay to feel.

For the Avoider

If you're an Avoider, you might be thinking, *"So, I'm avoidant. Why does that bother people and why can't they just accept that about me? Maybe this is the temperament I was born with and I'm just not a feeler? Why do I need to cry and feel my emotions for others to feel better about themselves? Sounds like their problem to fix, not mine!"*

I've heard many statements like this from Avoiders resisting recovery. They want to find a logical reason why it's okay to stay the way they are. Most Avoiders view looking back to childhood and parents for root causes of problems as excuse-giving. However, Avoiders are the kings and queens themselves of making excuses for not growing!

In my opinion, Avoiders are not the hardest style to be able to grow from, but the hardest attachment to be convinced to grow. All insecure attachments form from developmental injuries, and this is not how you are designed to be. Babies don't come out of the womb not feeling. You likely had some or all of the following experiences:

- As a baby you depended on your parents completely for your needs, but you may have learned to soothe yourself when they were not attentive or aware of what you needed. Your cries were not attended to, so you eventually stopped expecting them to respond.
- As a toddler you might have had to pick yourself up when you fell, or dealt with disappointment by yourself, and missed out on true comfort from a parent when you were scared, in pain, or angry. You may have been told to be brave because there was nothing to fear, to be strong like a big boy and not cry, or to calm yourself down because you were "whining."
- As a school-age child, you may have been left alone to take care of yourself or conditioned to accomplish tasks to get affirmations from your parents. If so, you essentially learned to perform to get the attention that you should have got unconditionally. By the time you became a teen or young adult, you didn't notice feelings of rejection or abandonment by your parents because you had been trained to ignore your emotions and not rely on others.

I understand it may be a challenge to get you to buy into seeing this cause and effect. You might tend to believe you are not being reactive because you don't yell, get outwardly upset, or say hurtful things back to others. Just because you *appear* calm on the outside does not mean you are not reacting on the inside. Many studies have shown that a calm, placid temperament alone does not predict a secure attachment. Calmness may help situations not escalate, but not yelling or arguing doesn't mean you aren't exacerbating unhealthy relationship patterns. It can sometimes be better to get upset on the outside, apologize, and make efforts going forward, than to remain forced-calm, not engage, and not make any growth efforts at all. The former demonstrates growth; the latter ensures stagnation.

From my experience, unlike the other insecure attachment styles, many Avoiders are *egosyntonic*—happy with how they are—because it continues to serve a purpose in some areas of their life. I've met many who recognize they were shaped, not designed, to be this way, but still have little desire to change. They reason, *If feeling my emotions more means I would feel anxious, sad, hurt, and bothered, why would that be a benefit to me?* If you don't feel the pain of your situation, it's because you are emotionally unaware.

I recognize that you might need to be logically convinced to learn emotional responses, which can seem like an oxymoron. But growing in attachment means you start to become more secure in being able to manage your emotions. Your resistance to emotions is because you fear having them, as your past experiences of emotions led to disappointment. That makes total sense. However, you will not be able to have close and intimate relationships with significant people in your life if you cannot connect emotionally. These relationships are likely suffering already.

Human brains are designed to use both logical and emotional aspects. Reasoning through logic alone may seem to you like the preferred way humans should act, but that's what robots do. Mankind has made amazing achievements using logic, but it's often the emotional responses, such as compassion and empathy, that people refer to as bringing out our "humanness." Only through allowing your emotions will you be able to fully understand yourself and others. Then you'll realize there's a whole side of life you've been missing out on.

For most people, emotions happen organically. But because yours were discouraged and you were conditioned to suppress and dismiss them, you need to find ways to feel again. Reconditioning will require intentionally practicing feeling each day and determining to stay in your emotions for an extended period. Learning about emotions and appropriate responses builds your emotional intelligence. But you also need to act on these insights to build **emotional competence**.

Ultimately, you will need to decide if you want to become secure and grow. Not growing though is also a choice. If you don't, then by default, you will be a parent who restricts your children from learning how to manage and respond to their emotions. This will possibly program them for disconnection with others and future relationship problems. You also will keep your spouse from fully knowing you, as well as keep you from fully knowing him or her. So, expect the problems that occur in relationships from lack of intimacy. And realize it will be hypocritical for you to blame others who also resist growing from their insecure attachment styles.

However, if you choose the path of growth and learn to access this repressed side of you, you will become a much more loving spouse, parent, and friend. You will realize the full extent of what positive emotions can feel like and see what you have been missing out on. Know, there are many recovering Avoiders cheering you on, and your future healed self is too.

You can do this!

REFLECT

1. If you have Avoider tendencies, how do you think your childhood shaped you to be this way?

2. Growing up, did you have a parent who was an Avoider? What impact do you think this had on your attachment to that parent and on your expectations about others meeting your emotional needs in adult relationships?

3. Is your spouse an Avoider? If so, now that you better understand how their insecure attachment style formed through a developmental deficit of not receiving enough emotional connection during childhood, what do you think you can do to help them practice connecting on a deeper emotional level? How can you begin to build compassion for the child they once were, who missed out on the emotional support needed to understand both their own emotions and yours?

4. Is one of your children showing signs of developing an Avoider attachment style? What factors might be contributing to this, and how can you support them in recognizing and connecting with their emotions more deeply?

Chapter Six

Pleasers Want to Help You Feel Better

When Noah was young, his mother had an undiagnosed mood disorder and experienced bouts of depression. If Noah and his brother were too loud, or rambunctious, their mother would head to her bedroom to "have a rest." When she'd retreat from the family in this way, the boys' father would blame them for *causing* her trouble. As the boys moved into adolescence, each reacted to the experience of their mother's intermittent absence differently. Noah's younger brother acted out by lying, stealing, and using drugs. But Noah felt more responsibility for his mom's mood, so he would walk the dog, and clean the house, and get straight A's on his report card trying to reduce stress for his mother.

To avoid feeling like the cause of his mother's retreat, Noah became a *Pleaser*.

Childhood Experience and Relationship with Parents

The Pleaser attachment style can form under several conditions:

- A parent is often angry, and their anger frightens the child.
- A parent is chronically stressed or depressed, and the child learns not to be another stressor.
- A parent is overly critical with high expectations, and the child feels not confident enough to perform.
- A parent is excessively worried and overprotective, and the child questions their own innate instincts in favor of their caregiver's sense of danger.
- A parent becomes emotionally dependent on their child to fulfill roles the parent should manage themselves—such as acting as a counselor during times of stress or serving as a primary source of joy to bolster the parent's self-image.

These types of dysregulated parents cause their children to feel anxious. Instead of the child's emotions being accepted and explored, and the child being soothed and comforted by the parent, the opposite occurs. The child learns to place their own emotions and needs as secondary and become compliant to manage the parent's stress reaction.

Pleaser children will develop a lack of confidence in their own abilities if they are not encouraged in normal developmental stages. They become codependent, constantly trying to calm their parent for them to feel safe.

> Pleaser children will develop a lack of confidence in their own abilities if they are not encouraged.

Pleasing and compliance become the child's main self-protective strategies to keep a stressed, angry, critical, depressed, or overprotective parent calm. Anxiety becomes the child's internal alarm bell to meet their parent's needs. The child monitors his or her parent's moods to predict the parent's needs, so that the parent stays regulated. This, in turn, helps the child to regulate themselves by producing calm and predictability as much as they can in their environment. This child can develop fears, worries, anxiety, clinginess, poor self-confidence, or performance anxiety due to regularly being in a state of hypervigilance.

A Pleaser attachment style can also form when properly managing conflict is not modeled for a child, and they are shielded from experiencing or observing ways to handle relational stress. These children have either passive parents who avoid conflict, or "helicopter" or "curling" parents who swoop in and rescue or smooth the path in front of them, so they don't encounter challenges. Unfortunately, these children are affected, because they don't build skill or confidence, remaining dependent.

Certain relational stressors are normal and necessary for healthy development (disagreements with friends, arguments with siblings, tensions with teachers, pushing against parental boundaries), so children who don't have these challenges miss out on vital developmental stages that are designed to help them navigate adulthood through resiliency-building. Parents who themselves have this attachment style typically have marital conflicts behind closed doors, or sometimes not at all, because this parent will give in to the other. Appropriately managing conflict, holding boundaries during tensions, and repair after ruptures are not modeled, so these important skills are not learned by the Pleaser child.

A child with a chronically sick or unruly sibling may also develop a Pleaser attachment style by observing their parents' ongoing worry and stress. To help keep tensions low, this child often takes on the role of "peacemaker" or feels responsible to be the "low stress child" to help out the struggling parent.

Pleaser children become the ultimate "good kids," not just in doing what is expected of them but also in temperament and behavior. And when the Pleaser child is labeled as "good," this approval reinforces the role. Avoider children are typically high performers because they are task-oriented and trained to be independent, but Pleaser children may become

> When the Pleaser child is labeled as "good," this approval reinforces the role.

high performers too, because that's the role of the "good student." They can appear self-motivated in school and compliant with teachers, which provides further reinforcement for being good outside of the home.

Common Views of the World and Relationships

When Noah grew up and married, he continued pleasing. Adept at noticing his wife's mood, he packed lunches, cleaned the house, and did laundry so she wouldn't be stressed and would be happy with him. He volunteered for assignments to win approval from his boss and church leaders, and hustled hard to ensure all his friendships were in harmony.

As an adult, the Pleaser's primary goal in relationships is safety, which they achieve by keeping others happy. Even if they are not consciously aware of it, Pleasers have been conditioned to be hypervigilant in reading angry, stressed, or disappointed body language. The Pleaser feels anxious when others are unhappy, so making others happy is really to reduce their own anxiety. Pleasers monitor people's moods to predict their needs like they did with their parents. And they will often neglect their own needs in favor of seeking peace and harmony to avoid negativity and conflict. Pleasers believe if they can regulate others, others will need them. Then they won't be rejected or abandoned and therefore are safe. So, when others appear stressed, Pleasers jump in to fix the problem or help the other person feel better. Having learned to be predominantly the giver and seldom the receiver in relationships, they expect little in return. Pleasers often rescue and caretake others, even when those individuals could benefit from learning to manage on their own. Over time, this dynamic leads to enmeshment in close relationships. Unconsciously, Pleasers tip the balance in their relationships to ensure they remain needed and are kept close.

Because most children will attempt to soothe their parents when they see them crying or sad, if the Pleaser was conditioned in childhood to take care of an overly stressed or depressed parent, they can become "empaths" in adulthood, taking on other people's pain. Difficulty saying no to others results in poor boundaries and overcommitment, consequently fueling their anxiety. Not wanting to disappoint others results in a lack of an established identity. If they had a parent who made decisions for them, some Pleasers may grow up second-guessing their own instincts. As adults, they'll often look to others to "copilot" their decision-making, relying on external input over trusting their own judgment.

The Pleaser's kind and giving nature and proximity-seeking is often attractive to other attachment styles (especially Vacillators and Controllers) who also seek closeness or submissiveness from others. Their low-conflict style can also make them attractive to Avoiders.

Common Internal Feelings

Anxiety is the Pleaser's dominant emotion, although because they have lived with it for so many years it has become their operating baseline. Some (especially high-performing Pleasers) may not be aware of it because feeling anxious is "normal" for them. Others notice their anxiety in the teenage years or early adulthood, when anxiety disorders typically develop. I've had many Pleasers tell me about having stomach issues in childhood with no apparent medical reason. It's only in adulthood they realize this was anxiety-related: When we are anxious our bodies shut down "rest and digest" functions as the sympathetic nervous system kicks in to put us on alert status.

Common Triggers

The Pleaser's main triggers are contained in the acronym SCAREDDD:

- **S**eparation (physically or in viewpoint)
- **C**onfrontation and **C**onflict

- **A**nger from others
- **RE**jection of their efforts
- **D**isapproval of them
- **D**isappointment from others
- Seeing others in **Distress**

The Pleaser's primary trigger is separation. Confrontation, conflict, anger toward them, rejection of their efforts, disapproval of them, and disappointment in them can all potentially lead to separation. Pleasers also feel anxious when others distance, want space, or won't talk about a problem. They interpret distance and silence as a sign that others may be angry or separating. Making decisions by themselves can cause anxiety that they may cause someone disappointment. And some extroverted Pleasers can be triggered by being left alone and will busy themselves so as not to be, which can cause overcommitment.

Common Conflict Patterns with Pleasers

Pleasers are proximity-seekers because they fear separation. They desire close connection because this means relational safety. They learn to rely on others' well-being to determine their own; clinginess and smothering is a common complaint from others in relationships with them. When others distance to avoid the smothering, Pleasers feel anxious and move closer, creating a cycle of distancing and pursuit.

When others are upset at them, the Pleaser's reaction to stress is to freeze or fawn (placate), rather than fight or flight. They have little ability to resist, and so they give in too easily. They pursue stronger, try harder, and give more in hopes of gaining acceptance and approval to calm their separation anxiety. If efforts to appease are not successful, they sometimes minimize or avoid the problem. Though they usually stay close, waiting for the other person's anger to recede. They have not developed an adult voice, so they often keep complaints to themselves and cover up their unhappiness with a smile or cheerful attitude.

Pleasers typically don't like to focus on negative things and will spin to the positive. For the Pleaser, negativity causes people to be unhappy and that triggers anxiety in them, so they want happiness, peace, and harmony to keep their anxiety at bay. Similar to experiences with Avoiders, when people are seeking empathy, but their emotions are minimized, or someone tries to "fix" their problem when that's not what they need, people feel dismissed. This is a common complaint about Pleasers, especially from spouses. Minimizing and avoiding negativity, and giving and appeasing to maintain connection, often results in others lacking respect for the Pleaser. Trouble saying no and little ability to resist pressure from others, especially when others act disappointed or upset at them, result in poor boundaries. Those who are close to the Pleaser can get frustrated with them, because the Pleaser becomes overcommitted and is unable to meet everyone's needs.

Many Pleasers are sensitive to their emotions and may cry easily. This is generally more socially acceptable for females. For male Pleasers, though, crying may not have been accepted by angry or critical parents, so if this was their experience, they may feel bad for crying and not find much relief in doing so.

Eventually, giving so much without receiving back can cause resentment, and Pleasers are vulnerable to burnout, especially around midlife. They can eventually leave relationships, but many wait decades before doing so. Others stay, giving in and placating to try and make things work, rather than working on their fears of abandonment and holding boundaries.

Reactivity in the Pleaser

The Pleaser attachment is characterized by fear and anxiety over upsetting and displeasing others, and an avoidance of conflict by freezing and pleasing. The freeze reaction is powerful and involuntary. When it is habitual, this is called learned helplessness, which is a sense of powerlessness resulting from persistent experiences of being unable to change one's circumstances.

Martin E. P. Seligman, an American psychologist, observed this phenomenon in dogs in the 1960s, as he sought insights into depression in humans. First, he and his colleagues took a group of dogs and administered electric shocks to them that the dogs could not predict or control, to see how the dogs would react to unescapable shock. Next, they repeated the experiment with this first group of dogs, and another group that had not undergone the initial experiment. This time, the dogs were put in a cage with a low divide that would be easy for each dog to jump over. When the shock came, the dogs that had not been in the first experiment quickly jumped to the other side and found it was safe. Conversely, many of the dogs from the first experiment simply endured the shocks without even trying to see if they could escape. Some even lay down in misery, conditioned to accept their uncomfortable circumstance as impossible to change. They had learned to be helpless.

Similar techniques are used in circuses on elephants, by tying a rope around the young elephant's leg to secure them to a pole. Once older, all it takes is a rope around the leg to keep the adult elephant from wandering, even though the rope is not secured to anything. A neural pathway of association between the rope and not being able to move has been built and reinforced, causing the elephants to believe they can't change their situation.

Pleasers have been conditioned to anticipate and reduce their parent's anger or stress to calm their own fear. Constantly being on the lookout for relational danger creates anxiety. There are different emotions under the category of fear. Fright is sudden and intense, and only experienced when the threat is present. Anxiety and worry encompass *potential* threats. Worry, though, is typically focused on a specific concern and experienced in the mind, while anxiety is a broader, more pervasive feeling of unease and is experienced in the body. Anxiety is typically a temporary state which we all experience at times in the face of fear or uncertainty. But, when someone is trained to constantly scan for danger, that anxiety can shift from being a passing feeling and become a chronic mental condition known as *trait anxiety*. In this state, the mind remains hypervigilant to *any* threat, and the body remains on the precipice of activation—ready to spring into survival mode as soon as a threat is identified.

Pleasers live with *trait anxiety*, and they experience frequent false-positive alerts from their amygdala, interpreting sometimes safe or neutral situations as threats. What the Pleaser needs in order to meaningfully reduce their anxiety is to retrain the sensitivity of their threat-detection system. However, instead of doing this deeper work, Pleasers often manage their anxiety in the short term by quickly mitigating perceived threats through submission and compliance. Alternatively, they may try to trick their amygdala into feeling safe by minimizing the depth of problem to themselves or avoiding it altogether.

Small children often freeze and fawn when faced with a threat because they are not fast enough to outrun the danger or strong enough to fight back. In childhood, the Pleaser's stress response system was triggered often, so that, despite being an adult, inside they still feel like a small child when facing danger. Some Pleasers might show some fight when pushed or run a little distance, but these responses are typically underdeveloped in them.

Creating Healthy Resolution with the Pleaser

Pleasers grow out of their fearful and hesitant approaches when they learn to own and confront their anxieties, establish their individual identity, assert themselves, and tolerate disapproval. Pleasers need a lot of affirmation and encouragement to learn to grow. And they tend to have a hard time doing the practical growth work, as fear is a strong primal driver. Their neural pathways are deeply embedded, and it will take time to establish new ones, which only occur through repetition of new experiences. Because they have learned to be helpless, their amygdala needs retraining to realize what are mild to moderate disturbances that can be tolerated and dealt with. Acting from primal survival, Pleasers are triggered by harsh anger and strong criticism. If you use these strategies to try and get them to change, you will continue to get the same results, as this only reinforces their programming. I see many spouses of Pleasers do this, especially spouses with Vacillator attachment styles, who then feel despair when it doesn't work. While our old neural pathways may never fully diminish, the responses we practice most often become the ones our brain defaults to over time. With consistent effort, new, healthier patterns can grow stronger and more automatic.

For them to grow, Pleasers need to know they are safe and free to share opinions and exert their feelings without risk of rejection. Help them discover their likes and dislikes with decision-making and positive support. *"How about you pick where we will eat today?"* Encourage Pleasers to voice what annoys them and share your support in setting healthy boundaries, even boundaries with you. Give them phrases they can use to say no to you so you know when they really don't want to do something. Let them know that if you are disappointed when they assert themselves, you will recover. Help prepare them to face others getting upset when they hold healthy boundaries, by telling them you expect them to hold their ground and not give in to you simply to keep the peace.

If the Pleaser can learn to do this with their spouse—in a relationship where they know that they will be loved and accepted and that healthy boundary-setting is not only okay but expected of them—they will learn to do this with others. That's the way it will work. If you want them to stand up for themselves to others, they must feel confident standing up for themselves to you. Our attachment healing only happens in a secure relationship. Once Pleasers feel secure in their bond with you, they can more easily be encouraged to set boundaries with others (parents, bosses, coworkers, friends).

> They must feel confident standing up for themselves.

What to Say to Engage the Pleaser in Self-Reflection or When They Get Fearful

Help them link their behaviors to anxiety:

"I notice that when (situation X) happens, you (do this behavior). I wonder if you feel anxious/worried that I will…"

Then ask follow-up questions to help them reflect on their reaction:

"How do you think that reaction will help you, me, or others become more secure?"

Validate and empathize with their anxiety, and encourage them to establish healthy boundaries and assert themselves by reassuring that you won't abandon them:

"I can understand why you feel anxious. What would you prefer to do? It's okay if I'm disappointed. It's a normal part of life."

If they try to pivot back to fixing, pleasing, or appeasing, remind them that growth is always uncomfortable. Remember, making healthy boundaries safe to set with you gives them a template to do it with others.

For the Pleaser

If you're a Pleaser, you're probably genuinely a nice person. Your spouse or your friends may say you're "too nice." And depending on the person, that either bugs them or they admire that about you. No matter, they likely agree you have poor boundaries. You may not understand what's wrong with being a nice guy or gal, or why others are bothered by it, but your pleasing causes you a myriad of issues.

I see many Pleasers coming to couples therapy saying they want to grow, but really what they want to know is how to please better or find the right words to say for their spouse to finally be satisfied with them. In reality, the opposite is needed. Growth will occur when you stop pleasing and become secure in who you are so you can tolerate displeasure from others. Pleasers are often drawn to a Vacillator spouse because both these attachments seek close proximity from a partner. No amount of pleasing or niceness is going to satisfy a Vacillator spouse. They want real over nice. So, you can keep trying the experiment but it's not going to work!

If you are a Pleaser wanting to grow and can't rely on those closest to you to support you in this process, you likely will need the help of a therapist as a neutral and secure attachment figure to encourage you and help you set boundaries. Since you are used to giving in to keep others happy, it will take a supportive figure to help you learn how to separate and *individuate*. Children can be helpful for feedback, but not emotional support. Even if they are now adults, this can too easily lead to enmeshment and parentification. Parentification is where a child is expected to take on an adult role in their parent's life, or roles are reversed in the relationship. Adult sons and daughters have their own attachment injuries, and this will not help them recover.

To enter recovery from your insecure attachment style, one of your first growth goals will be to learn to tolerate others being disappointed in you so you can accept and tolerate your negative feelings. Facing the thing that you struggle with, to gain a new experience, is the only way to recondition. To overcome anxiety, you need to learn to face threats, and distinguish if the danger is even real. Anxiety fades as confidence grows, so growing in confidence is the antidote. Once you feel confident standing against what your amygdala perceives as threats, and realize they are not insurmountable, anxious somatic symptoms will reduce. Exposure is the only way to overcome fears, and that will take great courage.

To combat your stress reaction system, the first step is identifying your triggers. When you feel the symptoms of the amygdala hijack, pause and notice what caused it. What are you fearful of? Is it someone's anger, disappointment, or disapproval? Or are you fearful someone you love is going to fail somehow? Labeling your triggers helps engage the PFC to take back control. Don't judge or label the situation "bad," just focus on this moment, not how you want to react, or past outcomes. Tell yourself: *"The threat in the present is not as great a danger as my body is telling me. I will be okay and this reaction will pass."* Try and see if you can make any links from your childhood to the feeling in the present.

If you had one dominant parent and one passive or somewhat absent-yet-loving parent who did not stand up to the dominant one, acknowledge this parent may have abandoned you in your time of need. They were the adult and should have showed you how to assert yourself. Because they didn't, that taught you when one person is dominant, others must submit. Some Pleasers struggle to acknowledge the failings of a parent they received love from who was only doing the best they could. Denying, minimizing, making excuses, or focusing mainly on the positive will only serve to reinforce these insecure pathways in you and will not lead to growth. You must acknowledge reality if you are to make sense of your childhood and build your coherent narrative. Acknowledging this parent's flaws is necessary to create cognitive dissonance and challenge you to do the work they maybe should have done.

Confrontation tends to be one of a Pleaser's biggest fears, but the only way to recondition yourself is to perform a different action. *Learn to confront the issue, rather than the person.* This makes it less personal and often less adversarial, because it shows you are not against them, but rather the issue itself. Begin with *"I want to resolve this issue..."* If you hit resistance, keep communicating that it's the impasse or circumstance that's the problem, not them:

"I'm feeling uneasy about the situation."
"I'm not sure that will solve the issue for me."
"I have an idea to see if we can solve this problem."

As you learn to confront, people will respect you more and this will help reduce further tensions or conflicts. Pleasers are liked because they are easygoing, but often they are not respected because of this. That's because others know you won't complain if they give you the "dirtier" job or the least desirable work assignment. Family members often try to keep the Pleaser in the role of "the good boy" or "the good girl," too, even in adulthood. When you view yourself as less deserving, this negative self-perception gives a green light to those who have a propensity to take advantage of others. But when you can see yourself as deserving, you will be more likely to hold boundaries. People also don't have to like your boundaries to respect them. Behaviors only exist in environments that enable them. You are not the cause of a person taking advantage of you, but by not holding boundaries and allowing disrespect you might be unwillingly reinforcing this behavior from others!

For growth to occur, you must change your relational patterns by facing your insecurities. You can wait for the problem to build and the conflict to come to you, or you can be in control of when a smaller conflict surfaces and address the problem before it escalates. If you wait for the bigger conflict, there will be more debris to wade through. Facing tensions is not a bad thing. We need tension to push against for any type of growth to occur, so expect resistance when you try and break a pattern. And when someone pushes back, it doesn't necessarily mean you're doing the wrong thing—it may even indicate that you're doing the right thing!

When setting and holding boundaries, phrase things in a way so the other person can see it's their actions causing the struggle, and you're acting *for you* rather than *against them*. Try some of these phrases: *"I'm not willing to be criticized and have my character attacked. That's not healthy for me. I'm willing to resume this discussion only when we can communicate our feelings in safe and respectful ways. I know it's possible to do this even if we're upset."* By using an "I" statement, you make it about your security, and by saying "we" in the expectation, you highlight a universal secure standard to be reached that you both have a part in. In this way, you make it clear where the other person's actions are causing a barrier to resolution. And because you include yourself in the standard, you show you are willing to do your part. If they don't comply, simply state your observation and reinforce your commitment. *"I can see you're not willing to communicate in this way yet. You can let me know once you are ready for both of us to hear each other out and resolve this."*

Remember, the primary goal in setting boundaries is not to convince the other person of your perspective, but to establish a limit. Boundaries are limit lines that have consequences for crossing them. It is not necessary for others to understand why you are holding a boundary for you to follow through on it. Respecting your limits starts with you enforcing them.

Consider your motivations as you grow, to make sure you are breaking the "please and appease" cycle. It's okay to be kind and do nice things for others, but ask yourself, *"Am I doing this to be liked and accepted because I fear disapproval, abandonment, or their reaction?"* If you have a pushy or demanding spouse, the negative feedback loop will continue until you are able to break the cycle and assert yourself. And if you are divorced, you owe it to your current or potential future partner to learn how to set and hold boundaries with your ex-spouse to protect your new relationship. **Whether you can learn to accept displeasure from others is going to be either the gatekeeper or the gateway to your growth!**

Caring about a person also doesn't require being involved in their circumstances. Pleasers often become entangled in others' emotional states. There is a difference between rescuing and supporting. Supporting is coming alongside and allowing others to learn to recover and build skills. Rescuing swoops a person out of a circumstance they've created and often robs them of the opportunity to grow by keeping them dependent on you. When you feel anxious over seeing someone struggle and want to help, try just empathizing with them instead. They may not even be looking for you to solve their problem. Focus on yourself and let them build strength by facing their problem. You will grow too by learning that you don't own others' problems. Emotions can be uncomfortable, but they are momentary. Remind yourself, they will pass.

A word of caution here: There are some people who are innately more sensitive than others. Dr. Elaine Aron, a clinical research psychologist, coined the term Highly Sensitive Person (HSP) after researching high sensitivity in people.[*] She identified that 15 to 20 percent of the population tend to have a nervous system with a higher sensory-processing sensitivity. Meaning, HSPs feel things more deeply and take longer to resolve physical and emotional pain, so stress can be more impactful on them. When an HSP develops a Pleaser attachment, they tend to absorb other people's pain and distress as if it were their own. And this takes an emotional, and often physical, toll on them. If you are an HSP or an introvert (or both), and you have a Pleaser attachment style, don't justify your insecure reactive coping strategies as part of your biological makeup. While an HSP's sensitivity is innate, it's possible to learn to be secure and build a tolerance to sensitivity when it causes you to have unhealthy or poor boundaries with others.

---

[*] Elaine N. Aron, *The Highly Sensitive Person: How to Thrive When the World Overwhelms You* (Broadway Books, 1996).

Finally, if you are married and have a critical or angry spouse who is harsh with your children, recognize that you have the *responsibility* to protect them. Don't abandon your children by being passive or deaf to the issue. Acknowledging and asking your kids to share out loud the hurts your spouse does to them is not a betrayal of your spouse. Not asking your kids may be a betrayal of them when you know they are hurting. Listening to them express their hurt or vent does not make you complicit in their complaining. Their complaints may be legitimate. You won't know unless you hear them out.

As a recovering Pleaser, assertiveness training or finding a codependency group can be a great help to encourage you, teach skills, and keep you accountable through this process. Or asking a therapist or trusted friend to role-play some common situations with you to build tolerance for confrontation.

As you practice you will get better, because this is how neural pathway-building works. Take heart, you *can* conquer your fears! I've seen others do it. Your new, healthier, confident self is waiting!

REFLECT

1. If you have Pleaser tendencies, how do you think your childhood shaped you to be this way?

2. Growing up, did you have a parent who was a Pleaser or a parent you were afraid of? Maybe you had a parent who was highly critical or chronically depressed? What effect do you think this had on your attachment to them and your anxiety levels in your adult relationships?

3. Is your spouse a Pleaser? If so, what do you think you can do to encourage them to not give in and tolerate your disappointment when they differ from you? How can you encourage their assertiveness, now that you know more about how their insecure attachment style stems from fearfulness and anxiety in childhood?

4. Is one of your children showing signs of developing a Pleaser attachment style? What factors might be contributing to this, and how can you support them in recognizing and managing their fearfulness so they can grow in confidence and emotional security?

Chapter Seven

Vacillators Long for More

Jonathan and Maria are both in their forties. Not long after they began dating, Maria learned that Jonathan had made the choice to not report all his earnings for his robust lawn-care business to avoid a large federal income tax bill. Last week, while she was at his house waiting for him to be ready for their date, she saw a letter out in the open on his dining room table from the IRS stating he was being audited. When she brought it to Jonathan, expressing concern, he snatched the letter and told her she was snooping and that "everything is fine." Maria was worried because she knew tax evasion could lead to jail time.

Later that evening, while dining together at a restaurant, Maria gently asked again. She had parents who modeled sharing stress and seeking comfort in one another. She was trying to do the same for Jonathan.

"I'm concerned," Maria admitted, "because I know you want to see your son graduate from college. I know you are trying your best to provide a good life for him. I'm sure this must be stressful for you."

Immediately triggered, Jonathan became agitated and pushed his plate away, flagged the waiter down, and asked for the bill. "I wasn't stressed until you just brought it up!" Jonathan snapped.

Maria, who was still getting to know Jonathan, didn't understand what had just happened.

Note that attachment styles prone to more outward demonstrations of anger and confrontation are often deemed "worse" than others because this can lead to physical and emotional abuse. However, all insecure attachments are dysfunctional, and each can be equally damaging to a person in different ways. Because the primary characteristic of the Vacillator attachment is ambivalence, this style has more facets and a wider variety of reactions than other styles. This chapter is slightly longer than the others for that reason, but not because the style is worse.

Depending on how dominant the style is in the person, some Vacillators may strongly identify with this whole description, while others only some. A big part of the challenge is that inner contradiction ambivalence creates. Ambivalence means having mixed or contradictory feelings. This can cause a lot of turmoil and shame, which Vacillators may either internalize as them being "all bad" or reject this because it feels too shameful to acknowledge parts of it. Many Vacillators have a high level of emotional functioning at times, and are often the initiators for seeking improvement in relationships. Other times, they are detached and they fluctuate between both these poles—hence the Yerkoviches' term, "Vacillator."

Childhood Experience and Relationship with Parents

Jonathan's parents divorced when he was four. He bounced back and forth in custody—one week with each parent. His father remarried and started another family. Jonathan's mother remained single and worked long hours. When staying with his mother, he was often home alone during the week until she got home from the office. When he was with his father, he felt out of place in the family. He was several years older than his half-siblings, and the household focus was on the stage of life his siblings were in. Even though both parents did the best they could, Jonathan often felt his needs were unseen.

The Vacillator attachment style is formed when a parent's attention is inconsistent, and connection only happens when the parent is available. Either this parent is unpredictable and is sometimes nurturing and responsive and at other times intrusive, insensitive, and emotionally unavailable; or this parent is not always physically available, so the child receives some connection but is left waiting and longing for more. This intermittent connection is experienced as a type of abandonment to the child, even if the Vacillator doesn't recognize that in adulthood.

Subtle abandonments can result from a parent being on military deployment, working untraditional schedules, being in and out of addiction, or devoting time to their own interests. Sometimes this attachment forms because the child has one passive but nurturing parent, who allows a more rigid and emotionally cold parent to set the house rules, so the child gets a mix of nurturing and rejection.

The bottom line is the child becomes anxious about when connection will occur, and no one is available to help them make sense of their feelings with language and empathy. So, the child protests to demonstrate their feelings by sulking, pouting, or having angry outbursts. They aim to show the parent their distress, creating a push-pull of "I want your attention, but I'm upset you made me wait for it," or "I want your love, but you are hurting me."

Common Views of the World and Relationships

Vacillators enter adulthood looking for the consistent connection they missed out on as a child. Their anxiety builds and turns into preoccupation about whether others are ready to connect, and ambivalence over desired outcomes. They're uncertain whether they want connection or repair, or are too angry to receive connection because they feel misunderstood or were made to wait for it. Their fear of abandonment, tangled with anger and shame over feeling unworthy of others' time, battle inside them.

Vacillators become idealists, longing for the perfect relationship free of hurt and disappointment to avoid the painful feelings of childhood. Anticipating unrealistic outcomes when relationships are new, Vacillators create idealistic versions of others in their minds. They often feel intense attraction at the beginning of romantic relationships. This can be incredibly exhilarating for the person who is being pursued with such fervor, and they are drawn toward the Vacillator because they may have never felt so valued and wanted.

Feeling anxious both in the excitement of connection and in the disconnection when their partner is away, Vacillators seek physical closeness as reassurance of the relationship's permanency. They confuse intensity for intimacy, often sharing too much, too soon—both physically and emotionally—in their anxiety to attach quickly. This often leads to deep disappointment when they discover their ideal was not real, at which point they may feel duped. When a relationship ends, the Vacillator's subsequent romantic pursuits then become an effort to re-create those feelings of excitement and exhilaration with the next person.

Common Internal Feelings

Vacillators experience their emotions deeply. When Jonathan blew up at the restaurant, he didn't *want* to be angry, though the feeling was intense inside of him. Anger can feel very strong for the Vacillator as a great sense of being wronged or unfairness rushes over them. Powerful feelings of being misunderstood lead them to intensely pursue their point, and hopelessness and despair can feel quite overwhelming, as it seems to them that others are never going to understand them and respond in the way they need. Their internal voice asks, *"Why don't others see what they're doing to me?"*

> Vacillators experience their emotions deeply.

Common Triggers

The Vacillator's emotional triggers usually come from the following primary feelings and can be remembered with the acronym MUDWARS:

Feeling **M**isunderstood
Feeling **U**nseen / **U**nheard
Getting **D**isappointed (from idealism)
Being made to **W**ait (especially for attention)
Perceiving **A**bandonment
Perceiving **R**ejection
Feeling **S**hame (from criticism, rejection, their own mistakes,
    or after acting poorly toward others)

These are core wounds developed in childhood when the Vacillators waited for connection, and felt abandoned and rejected doing so. Being left alone not knowing how to deal with their emotions caused them to feel unseen and unheard, which got reinforced if they had parents who did not hear them out. Feelings of deep disappointment and being misunderstood, knowing this was not how the parent-child relationship should be, led to longing for a more attuned connection, especially if parents couldn't validate or empathize with their experiences. Vacillators have two pathways to shame: feeling not good enough for others if they receive or *perceive* rejections and criticisms, and feeling inadequate when they make mistakes or if they have not lived up to their own standards by reacting in anger.

Common Conflict Patterns with Vacillators

Vacillators were conditioned in childhood to be outwardly focused by waiting on their parent to be available. In adulthood they remain hypervigilant to others' actions and skeptical that others will be available or reliable. They often perceive actions as rejecting or abandoning and as against them. Often these actions are minor. An example of perceived rejection could be not wanting to do something they want because you are too tired. And perceived abandonment could be as small as walking ahead when they have stopped to tie their shoe. When hurt, Vacillators push others away, or keep them at a distance, as a way to be in control of the impending separation they fear, thereby creating the very rejection or abandonment they are trying to avoid.

Idealization sets Vacillators up for disappointment since reality is never ideal. So, when something goes wrong, the Vacillator can feel like "everything is ruined," and become hurt and angry at the "spoiler." They place that person or thing in a "bad" category and start to internally devalue them.

Because they feel so wronged, this causes an overreaction. They believe their hurt is greater than others' hurt and that others don't see how wronged they were. This builds anxiety over feeling misunderstood and unseen. Vacillators often criticize and overexplain to be understood, which others may push back on because their hurts are not being acknowledged, or they don't agree they caused so much hurt to the Vacillator. Venting is a way for Vacillators to release anxiety, feeling better temporarily since they've "expressed" their feelings, even though it's often relationally destructive. These outbursts and protests are an attempt to bring restoration by getting the other person to see their pain, admit fault, and come after them.

When Jonathan blew up at Maria, his anger was masking shame over being found doing something wrong. Vacillators often don't recognize the vulnerable feelings (MUDWARS) driving their anger, and their words typically hurt others rather than encourage empathy for them. Blame and criticism push others away, and others may also struggle with how to respond to statements such as *"You're making me mad,"* which further disappoints the Vacillator. While the Vacillator's anger sabotages the connection, if others don't make efforts to take the blame and fix things they may be cut out of the Vacillator's life.

Vacillators are proximity-seekers but often don't like to directly ask for connection. Asking is vulnerable, and they perceive a no as a rejection—a pathway to shame for them. They also interpret someone not recognizing their needs as being unseen or unknown. For Vacillators, asking for their needs to be met can feel like it ruins the connection, as they expect all connection to be organic and feel "natural." Because they don't want to ask for their needs but still expect them to be met, they often criticize and complain in hopes others will notice what they need and respond. Even when others do respond, Vacillators can still reject the efforts, feeling disappointed they had to ask at all. If efforts don't feel natural to them, it means the effort wasn't real. They struggle to see that being willing to try, even when you don't feel like it, is often a loving response because it shows sacrifice.

Vacillators often tell others how to improve but don't like feedback themselves because it makes them feel defective (their other pathway to shame). Shame prevents the Vacillator from accepting mistakes, because waiting on connection from their parent made them feel not good enough to be connected with (especially if they were labeled selfish, ungrateful, spoiled, bad, or a brat), and making mistakes reminds them of this. While mistakes by others reminds them of being let down by their parent.

Reactivity in the Vacillator

The Vacillator attachment is characterized by anxiety over relational connections, preoccupation with hurts, and ambivalence over what they want. Anxiety occurs from anticipating future needs won't be met. Many times, Vacillators don't recognize anxiety because it's covered by their self-protective strategies, which typically play out in this common pattern, which I refer to as BADDProDD:

- **Blaming** others for hurt/disappointment
- **Anger** at the "spoiler"
- **Devaluing** to make the person "bad"
- **Defending** their behavior to avoid feeling shame
- **Protesting** to be understood and bring restoration

- **D**espair when protests backfire
- **D**etaching to relieve their hurt and anxiety

Rumination

Vacillators' anxiety builds from their MUDWARS triggers, which lead to preoccupation and ultimately venting as a way to release their anxiety. Their anxiety can also build from excitement. Because they fear disappointment, they struggle to wait and trust things will work out. They want the thing to happen right away so they're not let down so they can be impulsive. Their preoccupation with hurts or ideals results in rumination.

Vacillators ruminate in two ways: They rehearse upcoming or potential situations and review past interactions. When reviewing, Vacillators replay events in their heads, focusing on others' words or actions that could be interpreted as abandoning, rejecting, not understanding, or not seeing them. When rehearsing anticipated interactions, they forecast what others might say or do, and what they may need to do to self-protect, or get their needs met.

Things can only build for so long before they overflow. Seemingly ordinary or small events can cause the Vacillator's anxieties to come tumbling out, and often on an unsuspecting person. Others who are unaware of the Vacillator's rumination may be confused about what they've done to cause the Vacillator's strong reaction.

Vacillators use "emotional reasoning," which is interpreting one's feelings as facts. When they feel bad inside, they reason someone must have caused that, instead of seeing that a wound got triggered. Blaming others protects the Vacillator from their shame, but it also blinds them from seeing their core wounds.

Although Maria had just been curious to understand more about Jonathan, because he felt shame, he assumed she was the cause of him feeling bad, and he blamed her—first for snooping, and then later for causing him to feel stressed.

Protest and Push-Pull

Vacillators tend to see things as either being for them or against them (black-and-white thinking) and get hurt easily. Many Vacillators are not good at putting their hurt into words without it feeling like an attack or criticism of the other person. In conflict they become a prosecuting attorney, and others, especially spouses, may feel like they cannot match the Vacillator's quick attacks or comebacks to defend themselves or communicate their pain in a way the Vacillator will receive it. Vacillators can drive conversations into a cul-de-sac with no tolerance for others' opinions and yet no way to resolve. More introverted or milder Vacillators might feel sad and disappointed rather than angry and prosecuting. This leads them more toward withdrawal and hopelessness quicker, rather than pursuing to try and get restoration.

Conditioned to try to get others to notice and respond, Vacillators act out their feelings—sulking, stonewalling, withdrawal, distancing, withholding, or having an outburst. They want their needs met or an apology without having to directly ask. Unfortunately, the protests are typically hurtful, and the recipient may not be motivated to repair the damage.

Even when others are willing to seek resolution, the Vacillator can continue to push them away, feeling too angry or upset to accept the apology or efforts.

Despair

When the protest fails the Vacillator feels despair, thinking, *"Things are never going to change with them. It's hopeless!"* Vacillators get stuck in despair struggling to envision growth, as they view future outcomes from the lens of *how they currently feel*, rather than *how they can feel*. Despair keeps them from repair.

Detachment

When Vacillators don't get the reassurance they desire, they feel resentful. Detaching is the only way they see to relieve their pain. That's when you might hear a Vacillator say, *"I'm done!"* They diminish the other person to themselves as a defensive reaction through devaluing, and this becomes the vehicle they use for detachment. Devaluing plus rumination is a dangerous combination because it leads to bitterness and contempt. Many Vacillators have a trail of ended friendships that were suddenly amputated out of their lives.

The Shame Spiral

Of special note for Vacillators is their struggle to integrate good and bad. They tend to polarize by splitting people into "good" and "bad" categories with all-or-nothing expectations. Circumstances are fluid, and people have better and worse days, so the Vacillator can go back and forth in their assignments of people in these categories. They use confirmation bias by looking for either the good or the bad depending on how they feel. New and exciting relationships get idealized, and they can miss red flags. And disappointments and hurts can send them into the devaluing spiral, highlighting only the flaws of the other person.

Of course, this means Vacillators also struggle to integrate good and bad in themselves, and after outbursts and protests they usually feel intense shame. Even constructive feedback can send them into anxious rumination over mistakes and the shame spiral. Because they justify their actions and can be critical or harsh to others, people may not realize the Vacillator is just as critical and hard on themself. They typically struggle with secret shame. Their internal criticism is a private act they rarely share with others.

Many Vacillators don't apologize, because of this reason. Apologies are acknowledgments of mistakes. Making mistakes causes the Vacillator to feel defective, and so apologizing means they're "bad." Instead, they may try and balance out their bad actions by being nice to repair their self-image. If they do apologize, it can come with some justification of their hurt and anger, to reduce their shame and to seek to be understood.

The Vacillator's shame can make them acutely sensitive to challenges from a therapist to focus on their own growth when they feel wronged by others. Their anger feels justified to them, and so they can make lots of objections about why they shouldn't be the ones to change first, or they focus on why their angry feelings and reactions are valid and "anyone in their situation would feel this way." If they perceive a therapist to not understand them or to "call them out," Vacillators can end therapy abruptly, even after a long-standing relationship. It's not uncommon for Vacillators that seek therapy to cycle through many therapists over the years.

Reconnection Without Resolution

Detachment after a protest causes the Vacillator's feelings of abandonment anxiety to surface. Once their anger has dissipated, the Vacillator seeks closeness and connection that they can physically feel, to relieve this anxiety. They usually don't like to ask for connection out of fear of rejection, so they may reach out with a small gesture if they are not sure whether the other person is yet willing to reconnect.

This makes Vacillators more likely than other attachments to use "makeup sex" with partners as a substitute for relational repair. Physical touch is the most reassuring way to feel close connection, and sex is the highest form of intense physical connection a person can feel with a partner. While partners might be hurt from the conflict, they may enjoy the intense makeup sex and so move on without repair to not risk upsetting the Vacillator again. Without relational repair, pain gets stored away until the next upset. This unresolved pain then serves to amplify future hurts and reinforce the other person as "more bad" the next time.

At other times, spouses or other family members can just be glad the Vacillator has stopped protesting, and they don't have to walk on eggshells around them anymore. Rather than bringing up their hurt and risk starting the Vacillator's reactive cycle over, they move on too.

Unfortunately, when they've become entrenched in their defense mechanisms, and refuse to consider other's perspectives or work on their part in the conflict cycle, Vacillators can push people to see no other option but to end the relationship. If this happens, the Vacillator's abandonment anxiety can become stronger than their hurt. When faced with the choice to either make efforts to save a relationship or be left alone in their pain, growth can emerge—though often through an internal battle with resentment over feeling forced to change to avoid feeling abandoned.

Creating Healthy Resolution with the Vacillator

Resolution can be difficult with Vacillators because they are often too angry or hopeless to receive closeness. Spouses and family members must respond with an equal strength of security that matches the intensity of insecurity they encounter. You may be hesitant to do this as you understand how painful the BADDProDD pattern is for you all too well; however, the only way to end this cycle is for the Vacillator to learn to be challenged in a secure way. They need this resistance to push against in order to grow. And if you are fearful to do this, this is likely highlighting an area of growth in you as well.

> Resolution can be difficult with Vacillators because they are often too angry or hopeless to receive closeness.

What to Say to the Vacillator

Vacillators need to recognize their shame spiral, slow down to stop their reactive pattern (BADDProDD) so further hurts don't occur, and link their anger to vulnerable emotions (MUDWARS triggers) if they want to grow. It can be difficult facing strong anger and criticism from a Vacillator, but if you can remain calm and secure, they will be challenged to grow because they find it harder to devalue you when you respond in a healthy way. Try one of the following, depending on the situation:

> *"It's hard for me to know how to respond to your anger. If you can share with me a vulnerable emotion it will be easier for me to hear you without defensiveness. What hurt do you think is under your anger?"*
>
> *"I understand—you want me to know how you feel. It's overwhelming for me though to respond to multiple complaints. Please share with me what most hurt you."*
>
> *"Let's slow the conversation down so I can understand what you need. What hurt, sad, or fear emotions (from the emotions list) are you feeling?"*
>
> *"I see you and I want to help. Can you share with me what hurt you without blaming or accusing me?"*

Again, be prepared for resistance. A Vacillator may not like being slowed down because it can trigger feeling unheard. However, an angry Vacillator must not be allowed to simply "vent" on people. This does nothing to heal the hurt or change your dynamic. The above invitations communicate a willingness to listen if they can productively share vulnerable emotions. Reassure them they can have influence over being heard and understood if they can manage their reactivity and communicate securely. They also must be willing to take turns and accept you may not agree:

> *"I can see that you're mad about this, but I know we can communicate our feelings and perspectives in safe and respectful ways, even if we disagree."*

> *"We are both hurt. I'll go first and listen to your feelings if you can agree to then listen to mine in the same way."*
>
> *"I may not agree with you, but I do care about you so I will try and understand what it is you are feeling. Afterwards I would like to take a turn to share my feelings and be heard even if you don't agree with my perspective."*

Notice these are now statements rather than questions. If the Vacillator is too angry to be redirected to engage, or you hit a dead end in the conversation, you may have to temporarily call for time out:

> *"This isn't working very well. I want to understand, but it is hard for me to listen when you are this angry and attacking. I know you may feel abandoned if I leave without hearing you out, so I will check back in twenty minutes, and we can try again."*
>
> *"I can see you are upset about this and that this is important to you, but I'm not willing to argue or be yelled at. If you can calm down and speak respectfully, I will listen now. Otherwise, let's try again when we can both listen to each other patiently and respond kindly. I'm not going anywhere, but let's check back in twenty minutes and we can try a do-over or you can let me know when you are ready."*

Since Vacillators are abandonment-sensitive, **always give a timeline for when you will return** to pick up the conversation.

And if you're feeling too triggered, try something like:

> *"I'm feeling triggered, and I need a few minutes to calm down so I can listen and respond in a better, more secure way. I am going to gather my thoughts and compose myself. I should be ready in about twenty minutes if you are willing to try then."*

Once you've heard them out, validate any vulnerable emotion so they know you see their hurt even if you disapprove of the way they initially reacted. You might say:

> *"I can understand why you did that now."*
> *"I would be hurt too if that was my perspective."*

Then, help them form a request based on their needs. That might sound like:

> *"Given how you feel, what do you need from me to help?"*
> *"Can you change your complaint into a request? That will make it easier for me to respond."*

Again, do not take all the blame in a situation just to appease. This only reinforces the pattern and won't lead to your growth or theirs. To break the shame spiral, the Vacillator needs to recognize it by learning to receive negative feedback without defensiveness. You will have to be strategic to help them see you are not making them "all bad" as you voice your concerns. Acknowledge any good you see in them before you give your feedback. I understand this may be hard if you are being criticized. Think about the qualities in them that you appreciate. If you can't think of anything, then acknowledge their intention to want to improve the relationship. **It's the relationship you are affirming, not their behavior.** Integrating the positive and negative in people will require *modeling* that you can accept this in them as well as in yourself. Try this:

> *"I can appreciate that you want us to be connected and that you want us to improve. Because I love you and our relationship is important, I would like for us to solve this too. I don't like fighting with you, and I think you feel the same. My desire is for us to be able to work out hurts in a way that is constructive*

so we can be more attuned to each other's needs. Can I share with you where I feel hurt?"

Press in for fairness. An angry Vacillator who voices their hurts must then be willing to listen to your response. If they dismiss your feelings, highlight this as a double standard and point to a universal standard that you both should be reaching for. Use phrases like:

"I'd like you to listen to me <u>in the same way</u> you want me to listen to you."
"I know you wouldn't want me to do <u>that same thing</u> to you."
"I know you would want me <u>to do the same</u> for you."

You may have to set these expectations before they share. After you have listened and shared with them, help them notice their self-protective strategies:

"I notice that when <u>(this situation)</u> happens, you do (mention behavior). I wonder if you feel (guess a vulnerable emotion from MUDWARS) in those moments and need (give the corresponding need)."

Then tell them a more productive strategy for how they can communicate to get their need met:

"When you feel (emotion), if you can say (give a productive phrase), I will respond."

Some Vacillators may need stronger boundaries. Acknowledge their feelings but hold firm and put responsibility on them to respond appropriately. If they are sulking, try saying:

"I love and care about you but it's hard to respond when you don't clearly tell me what you need, and you act hurt and mad at me. I'm willing to be open to and consider resolutions. Please let me know when you are ready to make a request."

Most Vacillators I have met appreciate these phrases. However, if they're annoyed by them, don't give in. These phrases reflect the power they have to get their needs met and are in the best interests of them and your family. Part of the Vacillator's healing is to build tolerance for hearing things they don't like. Part of your healing from your own insecure attachment style may be to learn to say phrases like these and build tolerance for accepting displeasure from the Vacillator.

The Vacillator needs someone to help ground them when they are upset, because this is what they missed out on as a child. To do this they need strong and secure boundaries to push against to challenge them to grow, along with acknowledgment you see them and their pain. Practice communicating care for them in an authoritative and loving way and you can help them take responsibility for their growth and work through conflict.

For the Vacillator

I personally understand what it's like to be a Vacillator and be challenged to grow. Your feelings are strong because your wounding is deep, and that doesn't feel fair. As a child, you didn't feel important, or you were abandoned, or rejected, and it seems like this is continuing to happen in your current relationships. When you become aware of the vulnerable emotions (MUDWARS) under your anger and recognize hurts in the present feel stronger because your core wounds are being triggered,

> Recognize hurts in the present feel stronger because your core wounds are being triggered.

you can depersonalize interactions. Reining in your reactivity (BAD-DProDD), and learning new phrases to share your hurts and request for your needs productively, will help you build new pathways to get the closeness you want. As you learn these things, I promise, you will react less, and your triggers will diminish.

You will never be happy staying as a Vacillator. There's nothing wrong with hoping for a more fulfilling connection, but because you tend to idealize, you will always be left longing for versions of things that cannot be reached. And because you are ambivalent, you will always be changing your mind on what you want.

Don't let these childhood wounds keep grabbing your adult steering wheel and veering you off the path to secure attachments. Pushing others away or threatening detachment will not produce closeness. Disagreements are normal in relationships. The goal of a good relationship is not to avoid ever getting hurt or disappointed, but to learn how to connect in our differences. Secure individuals hear each other out, seek understanding rather than demand agreement, and repair when ruptures happen. To do this, you need to learn to accept and tolerate your negative feelings. Both pleasant and unpleasant feelings are part of being alive. Learning to manage them means we are comfortable being human.

Also, ambivalence is being stuck in two minds about where your happiness lies, which ultimately keeps you from being happy. If you want to overcome it, you must let one feeling win. Or another solution is learning to accept the good and bad in life and still be content. Life is not always fair, and people don't always behave as we would like them. To acknowledge this is to accept the reality of being in community. Everyone has a growth curve, including you. Facing and acknowledging the consequences of your actions and repairing ruptures are what you need to form an integrated view of yourself and others. Once you can accept good and bad in yourself, you can accept good and bad in others. This will help you reduce idealization and give yourself and others grace.

Notice when you are ruminating or being preoccupied with something, and how this builds anxiety or drives shame in you. And recognize your devaluing is leading to your feelings of resentment and despair, which drives your rumination. Gratitude is a good antidote. Look for the good to find a healthy balance in your temporary feelings. Feelings are not facts. They should be indicators, not dictators. Feeling disconnected doesn't mean you actually *are*. Likely, a wound is being triggered. When you can manage your emotions and self-soothe, your feelings will subside. And when you can release your shame, you will see you have no more problems than the other insecure attachment styles and just as much opportunity to know security.

Being a recovering Vacillator, you may think I'm biased here, but Vacillators can make some of the fullest recoveries into an earned secure attachment because they are not afraid to feel emotions, they pick up on changes in the moods and feelings of others, they are hopeful for relationship improvement, and they are usually not afraid to speak the truth.

Their tendency to ruminate can also hold an advantage to developing the observing self if they can shift their focus from being fixated on how others hurt them, to examining what they are feeling and why they reacted like they did. I've seen many recovering Vacillators show remarkable growth. And because of all of this, they also make for great therapists!

REFLECT

1. If you have Vacillator tendencies, how do you think your childhood shaped you to be this way?

2. Growing up, did you have a parent who was a Vacillator or one who was intermittently available? Or did a parent die or leave? How do you think this experience affected your attachment to that parent and shaped your expectations of others in adult relationships—especially regarding their willingness or ability to connect with you and meet your emotional needs?

3. Is your spouse a Vacillator? If so, how do you think you can acknowledge the pain beneath their anger or hopelessness while maintaining boundaries and not getting caught in their push-pull behavior—especially now that you understand their insecure attachment likely comes from real or perceived childhood abandonment?

4. Is one of your children showing signs of developing a Vacillator attachment style? What factors might be contributing to this, and how can you provide the consistency they need while helping them recognize and manage their preoccupation with hurts, ambivalence, idealization, and disappointment?

Chapter Eight

Controllers and Victims Facing Their Unsolvable Struggle (Disorganized Attachment)

Stephen was twelve when his mother remarried a man who was secretly a cocaine addict. His stepfather, insecure and intimidated by Stephen, was unnecessarily rough with him. In his periods of withdrawal from his addiction, he could be particularly mean. Stephen wanted to protect his mother, and his younger sister, Julie, from their abuser, but was ultimately helpless. Silently, in bed one night after getting a black eye for his efforts to turn his stepfather's anger away from his mother and sister, Stephen vowed he'd never be a victim again.

And he wasn't.

Growing up in chaotic homes doesn't always lead people to imitate or allow abuse. This may depend on the severity of their trauma. It can also display as a mix of the other insecure styles, depending on what seems most protective for that relationship or circumstance. If you have close relationships with people who present either authoritarian or passive tendencies—identified here as the Controller and the

Victim[*]—it's important to know how these styles form and find each other. While these aren't the traditional designations in attachment therapy, they help differentiate how Disorganized attachment can create two seemingly opposing, tumultuous patterns.

The use of the names Controller and Victim in this description are meant to be descriptive of the pervasive bonding style, not meant to be interpreted with the negative connotations of being a victim of abuse or wanting control. Because a person is a victim of a crime, this does not mean they are weak or something is wrong with them. Many personalities or attachment styles also like control. Avoiders are independent and may like to be in control of outcomes because they believe they can't rely on others. Pleasers are fearful and like to control their surroundings to stay safe or not be abandoned. Vacillators like control because they are idealistic and don't want to be disappointed. Wanting control is not in itself a bad thing. Controlling others by abusing them is.

Childhood Experience and Relationship with Parents

Disorganized attachment occurs when a caregiver becomes a source of ongoing major stress or danger to the child, or exposes them to an abusive environment. Abuse can take many different forms—physical, sexual, emotional, psychological, or neglectful—and may happen knowingly or unknowingly. Unknowing abuse can come from a parent's diminished mental capacity, or ignorance of nurturing practices, or simply unawareness that a babysitter, family member, or another child is a perpetrator. Chaotic environments can also occur when a parent has an addiction or mental illness (personality or mood disorder), causing them to be volatile and unpredictable in their care.

---

[*] Milan Yerkovich and Kay Yerkovich, *How We Love: A Revolutionary Approach to Deeper Connections in Marriage* (WaterBrook Press, 2017).

In these environments, the child becomes overwhelmed and confused and can't trust their safety or physical needs will be provided for. A Disorganized response grows out of the need to both escape the danger the parent allows, and yet remain close to the parent for basic provision, leaving the child with an unsolvable problem and no clear adaptive strategy to keep themselves safe. These primal needs for safety and attachment conflict and create the "disorganized" reaction of *approach-avoid behavior*, coined by Mary Main in her continuation of the "Strange Situation" trials.

> These primal needs for safety and attachment conflict and create the "disorganized" reaction.

Children with Disorganized attachment may have periods where different attachment strategies work, if the abuse is intermittent throughout childhood or situations change. An abuser may leave for a while, or the child might move to a different setting such as foster care or living with another family member. Yet a Controller learns that their most adaptive strategy is fighting back against a threat to make it stop. They learn relationships are control or be controlled, and that unpredictability leads to danger. They control their environment through dominance of people. While Stephen became a Controller, Julie formed a Victim attachment. When Stephen's family was at the dinner table, and the yelling began, Julie sat silent, frozen. After dinner she'd retreat to her bedroom and hide in the closet until the chaos stopped for the evening. Stephen left the house at sixteen years old, and when he did there was no one to protect Julie.

Someone with a Victim style finds freezing and staying small and silent is most adaptive until the danger is over. They believe if they can remain unnoticed, maybe the danger won't find them this time. At other times, danger is unescapable, and they learn resisting is futile. Victims often dissociate in unescapable threat. This is the mind's adaptation in order to separate emotional trauma from the physical abuse by disconnecting from the present. It typically results in fragmented or no narrative memory of an incident, though a physical reaction (implicit memory) still gets stored in the body.

Jesse came to see me because she'd just gotten married but couldn't relax during sex. I asked if she had a history of sexual abuse, and she told me that one of her mother's boyfriends would come into her room and sexually abuse her when she was three years old. Yet she had no memory of the abuse, and only knew because her mother eventually lost custody for failing to protect her from these and other incidents.

Adrenaline, chaos, and high intensity are usually ever-present in abusive environments, so these children can become thrill-seekers or numb to feeling, conditioned to think high adrenaline or simply surviving are "normal" states. Many children raised in these environments, like Stephen, leave home as soon as they can provide for their basic physical needs.

Common Views of the World and Relationships

Controllers and Victims learn that relationships have volatile power dynamics. Controllers look for someone they can control, and they often find a Victim who is used to being controlled. These styles are not gender-specific or socio-economic class-specific. Females can become Controllers and males can become Victims. People with these styles can even be highly educated. In the case of Stephen's family, Julie dated a string of abusive men. But Stephen? He married a woman who was submissive, and had children whom he controlled. Controllers make and enforce rules for others in an authoritarian way, so they won't be threatened or abandoned. They want to stop threats before they can occur, and they use bullying and intimidation to stay in charge. Chaos in childhood was normal, and so being in charge of it can create a natural high for them. Rather than avoiding danger, Controllers often engage in risky behavior and criminal acts. However, not all

Controllers are physically abusive. Stephen despised the physical abuse his stepfather did to him. He never hit his family, though he barked orders and was scary, repeating some of the same humiliating messages to them he heard from his stepfather.

Victims have learned to survive, but they are different from "survivors." Survivors have grown stronger and more resilient from their challenging circumstance and are now thriving. They feel empowered by having overcome their experience, where Victims continue to be bound by the past, not progressing toward growth. Because danger was ever-present, Victims are passive and even allow danger, tending to accept it as "normal." They often are not equipped to be good protectors of their own children, since children rely on their parents' sense of danger to teach them and keep them safe. The Victim's obliviousness to danger or lack of agency to change their circumstance can be frustrating to others who try and help them. It's also understandable for outside observers of this dynamic to be angry toward the Controller for seeming so cruel. Neither are intentionally like this; in surviving the chaos they were exposed to and not experiencing the safety love provides, these are simply the lessons they have learned about how relationships are.

> Victims are passive and even allow danger, tending to accept it as "normal."

Common Internal Feelings

Shame and powerlessness from the atrocities that happened to them as children constantly lurk beneath the surface for the Controller and Victim. Because the Victim has no self-agency, they may feel hopelessness, resulting in depression. Controllers never want to feel vulnerable again, so they keep shame from surfacing with their anger as it makes them feel powerful. Controllers may also experience depression, though it's harder to recognize because it displays in anger, rather than sadness.

Disorganized attachments often feel extreme internal reactions to stress triggered from their childhood history. Both Controllers and Victims may disassociate, self-neglect, self-harm, have suicidal gestures, engage in risk-taking, act out sexually, or use alcohol or drugs to numb their feelings.

Common Triggers

Reminders of powerlessness and shame are both the Controller's and Victim's triggers. Anger from others triggers these feelings for the Victim, as they default back to their childhood survival state of freezing and dissociating. Criticism and assertiveness from others trigger these feelings in the Controller. Controllers interpret these as a challenge of their authority and a threat to their control of their environment—not having a sense of control led to humiliation and shame in childhood. Instead of feeling relaxed when things are calm, both Victims and Controllers often feel anxious. In chaotic environments, calmness is rare and often precedes chaos, like the calm before a storm. Usually, during periods of calm, adrenaline builds, and both can become agitated.

Common Conflict Patterns with Controllers and Victims

The Victim may usher in "the storm," seeking to get the anxiety of an impending outburst over with by provoking the Controller. During conflict or abuse the Victim numbs to dissociate from the pain and shows little resistance. The Victim's relational goal is to be taken care of because they don't know how to take care of themselves. Because they have learned to comply for safety and survival, they often accept the blame for problems. Victims have developed a learned helplessness from experiencing fright without solutions. They learned to tolerate the intolerable as a child, and continue to do so as an adult. They weren't allowed to have opinions or be heard when they were younger, so they have not developed their adult voice. They did not receive compassion from their caregiver, so they lack sympathy for themselves and often believe they are unworthy and unlovable.

In conflict, the Controller rages and intimidates to get others to fall in line and stop the perceived relational threat. The Controller's relational goal is to maintain control and stop their childhood feelings of powerlessness from arising, so they never feel shame again. The Controller's rage is typically sudden, intense, and frightening, and they may become physically or emotionally abusive, humiliating others to get them to quiet down. They imitate the abuse done to them in childhood because they have learned these tactics have immediate effect.

After angry outbursts, some Controllers may become fearful of abandonment or feel shame over their destructive behavior, and they can appear remorseful and even kind for a period to woo back the casualty of their rage. In this state, Controllers can make promises to change, yet they tend to lack sympathy for others because they lack it for themselves. So, their remorse is more about shame reduction and self-preservation than relational repair or empathy.

Controller and Victim Attraction

The Victim is naturally attractive to the Controller because their lack of boundaries and submissiveness make them easygoing during the courting period. The Controller sees they can make all the decisions with no pushback, and this feels safe to them. Other dominant or rescuing types like the Vacillator and Pleaser can also be drawn to the Victim.

> The Victim is naturally attractive to the Controller.

The Controller is attractive at first to other attachments, not just Victims, because during the courting period they appear protective, decisive, and eager for closeness. They can seem to want intimacy, but the motivation for closeness is to monitor the person at all times to prevent abandonment. As the relationship develops partners eventually feel smothered. During the courting period, Controllers might demonstrate more ability to restrain their temper until they know the other person is bonded to them. However, once their partner is bonded, their rage more freely comes out. The Controller can swing from being sweet to being cruel, often isolating partners from family and friends to make them more dependent financially or socially, so it is more difficult for the partner to leave.

Growing up in a chaotic home, touch was often frightening and intrusive, rather than soothing, gentle, or nurturing as it should be. Neural pathways may have been wired for the Controller and Victim to expect or need adrenaline to feel connected, even for perceived intimacy. The Controller controls that adrenaline flow now, and they create the intensity. They can become masochists, demanding painful and humiliating sex acts from their partners.

Physical touch paired with adrenaline often feels normal to Victims, and they may endure violent or humiliating sex acts to prove their "love." Because their caregiver was the source rather than the reliever of stress, Victims have no example of what secure and healthy connection should be like. And because adrenaline is such a powerful bodily feeling, it can be mistaken for deep connection. Intense makeup sex after a destructive fight can feel so exhilarating to both parties that the destruction from the fight is quickly overlooked.

Helping Controllers and Victims

Many people are willing yet feel unequipped to help these attachments. For the Victim, the strategies for healthy resolution are similar to those used with the Pleaser: helping them discover and use their adult voice to verbalize needs and then set and hold healthy boundaries. With the Controller, resolution looks similar to the Vacillator, helping them self-reflect on the fear and shame under their anger, and to accept others' right to hold appropriate boundaries. The main differences are that the Victim and Controller will likely need to do significant individual recovery work for these efforts to be truly collaborative, due to the trauma they've endured. This can make these attachment styles harder to overcome. Victims who dissociate or pretend everything is fine are less willing or available to receive help from others. And Controllers who are physically abusive can make it dangerous for others to risk confronting them about their behavior or to suggest they get help.

Below, I will outline some steps each can take to seek healing, but first we need to see how someone with *any* attachment style can become a victim and willingly stay with an abuser.

Trauma Bonding and the Cycle of Abuse

For those who have never known the intensely disorienting experience of relational trauma, watching people you care for stay in and perpetuate abusive situations can be confusing and frustrating. Why would anyone endure abuse, let alone go back to an abuser, especially when it seems like they have the support and resources to break free?

An internal draw toward an abuser is formed from the chemical power of our hormones. You don't have to have a Disorganized attachment style or come from an abusive home to become a victim of an abusive relationship. All the insecure attachment styles can get caught in the cycle of abuse. Victims and Pleasers are more likely to because they push back the least and have learned helplessness. Vacillators can also become emotional abusers when they are chronically irritated and verbally aggressive, yelling at and shaming others to get their way.

Abusive relationships often do not start out abusive, and there are several phases identified in the conditioning of the person to stay. Chaotic relationships usually start with a courting period that's not yet chaotic. The future abuser will shower the future victim with affirmations, compliments, gifts, and intense acts of love and affection. Known as "love bombing," this feels exhilarating for the receiver, especially if they were abused or felt abandoned or alone as a child. After this comes the "dependency-building" stage, where the abuser gets the victim to solely rely on them by isolating the victim from others. The abuser manipulates the victim into giving them more attention and doing things for them, while discouraging spending time with, or doing things for, family or friends. Or the abuser takes care of all the victim's physical and financial needs to create a dependence upon them, sometimes even encouraging the victim to quit their job to create financial dependence.

Abusers create a power dynamic, and once this is established, the abuser slowly shifts toward criticizing the victim. Most romantic relationships have an infatuation stage where partners overlook minor offenses or inconsistencies, before each person shifts to a more realistic view, and conflict begins to occur. But with traumatic bonding, a power imbalance develops within which only the abuser is allowed to express criticism, while the victim gradually learns to suppress their own needs and conform to the abuser's expectations—often because they've become financially dependent or rely on the abuser for their sense of self-worth. In the "criticism stage," the abuser offers affirmation only when the victim does things for the abuser, and criticizes when the victim does things for themself or others.

> Abusers create a power dynamic.

When the victim questions these criticisms as unrealistic expectations, the abuser gaslights them by denying, pleading ignorance, and making out that the victim is the abuser or a controller of them. These conversations often end up in loops with no way for the victim to explain themselves or challenge the abuser. If the victim has been successfully isolated from friends and family in the dependency stage, the victim is less able to validate their doubts. The abuser conditions the victim to doubt their own perception of reality, often leaving them feeling as if they're going crazy. Due to emotional—and frequently financial—dependence, the victim comes to believe the abuser. The victim tries harder to meet the new standard, but soon becomes emotionally exhausted, anxious, and eventually depressed. They don't know what went wrong or why their great efforts backfire, and they hold to the hope that the exhilarating feelings they once felt about the relationship may return, which they temporarily can when the abuser decides conditions are acceptable.

It's usually once this stage is set where the abuse starts to occur. When the victim begins to show signs of readying leaving or giving up, the next stage of "intermittent reinforcement" begins to maintain the trauma bond. The abuser may apologize, make promises of change, or "reward" the victim with positive behaviors and love bombing again. The victim is reminded of the person they fell in love with and the side of the person they are desperately trying to get back, and they temporarily feel hope this can happen.

In trauma bonding, our primary bonding hormone, oxytocin, and our stress hormone, cortisol, combine with our action hormone, adrenaline, and our reward hormone, dopamine. All get chemically joined to send the most powerful and confusing internal messages to the brain about whether the abuser is "good" or "bad" for them. For people with Victim attachment styles, these are familiar feelings from childhood they had toward caregivers. The victim gets addicted to the high of love bombing, which is often enough to keep them sustained even during the low of abuse. A similar reaction happens in the brain with the high and low of drug and alcohol addiction.

Addictions cause cravings and withdrawals, and in trauma bonding, the feelings the abuser's love bombing provides are the drug. Emotions are alogical—meaning they don't always follow logic or reason. Similarly, hormones like dopamine, oxytocin, and adrenaline are values-neutral—they simply respond to what the brain perceives as meaningful or rewarding. Dopamine is released whether you're doing something beneficial, like exercising, or harmful, like cocaine. We can bond through oxytocin with people who are both safe or harmful for us.

And adrenaline gets released in excitement as well as during stress activation. Addictions are powerful, so the victim typically makes excuses for staying in the relationship.

Some abusers may genuinely feel guilt and shame over their actions, which is the driving force behind their apologies and commitments to change and why victims believe them, because the remorse is real. They may view their love bombing as a genuine way of showing affection, and abuse as their way of demonstrating dissatisfaction, because they only know how to relate to others with intensity and adrenaline. People usually become this way because adults who should have been trustworthy taught them that feeling adrenaline, cortisol, dopamine, and oxytocin all at once was what it means to be in a relationship. Child sexual abusers do this to children. They "groom" them, abuse them, then threaten or tell them, "You wanted it too," or "You made me do it," to keep the child locked in the abuse cycle.

Whether the Victim and Controller style is predominant or not, both parties tend to deny and minimize or cover up the abuse hoping for things to get better. Abused people often caretake their abuser when the abuser is feeling deep guilt and shame in periods of remorse. Some victims recognize abuse but still won't leave because they feel so emotionally bonded, and/or trapped by finances, faith beliefs, or fear of leaving children in split custody with the abuser. Abuse does not have to involve physical or sexual mistreatment.

By themselves, the following can also be types of abuse:

- Financial (controlling your access to money or how you spend it)
- Spiritual (using scripture to justify controlling or manipulating behavior, or to guilt you)
- Emotional (put-downs, mind games, intimidation, taking your property, threatening you)

- Isolating (controlling where you go, monitoring your phone calls, texts, or emails, or limiting your access to friends and family)
- Mental (gaslighting, minimizing abuse, shifting blame, playing victim, falsely accusing you of cheating)

For Victims

Safety is paramount if you are in an abusive situation. Healthy relationships have boundaries and reciprocity, and this balance must be restored for you to grow. **Couples therapy is not recommended when there is active abuse.** Although it may seem like a good idea, especially if your abuser suggests it, therapy confronts uncomfortable feelings and situations. Though your partner may temper their anger during the session, you may suffer their wrath afterwards if they felt exposed. Or they may use what you have shared vulnerably against you to continue to manipulate. When you fear speaking up, future sessions become less honest and this will only reinforce learned helplessness in an environment where you should feel safe. Particularly with violent abusers, recovery work is best started in an individual setting. They need to learn better ways to express and manage their emotions and behaviors before others can be invited to grow with them.

To break free from the abusive cycle, victims must first recognize what's happening as abuse and then decide they won't put up with it anymore. It's hard to grow in a storm, and so depending on the severity of the abuse, a separation may be necessary. Though it may not feel like it to the abuser, separations are in the best interest of both partners' growth. If you do not feel safe, have this conversation in a public place, over the phone, or with a third party present. Always tell someone if you are going to have this conversation and when it will happen so they can check on you.

You don't need to have a decision made on whether you're going to work toward reconciliation with the person if you decide to separate from them. It's okay to be "on pause" and not have all the answers yet. The initial goal of a separation is to get to safety so you can get perspective and begin to assess what's healthy for you. You also don't need to give the person a timeline for when you'll make your decision. Time alone doesn't guarantee growth. Growth occurs by the amount of effort a person puts in. I recommend making decisions in six-month increments and starting timelines for monitoring growth for when the abuser enters recovery. From periods any shorter than that, it is difficult to know if growth efforts can be sustained. The abuser may want to know these things up front, but the unknown of these answers is the tension they need to motivate them to **grow for themselves**, not just to win you back. Transformation only truly occurs when our motivation is internal. If it is external only, you can't know if behavior will revert once circumstances change. You deserve a safe and loving relationship, and should accept nothing less.

I understand having a separation from someone whom you've been in a relationship with for a while can be scary because, while you also have growth to do, there is an "unknown" factor that it is dependent upon their ability to grow for your relationship to improve. There may also be logistical factors of where you or they will live and how finances will be shared. However, if you don't address the cycle, it will only continue and may even get worse, making it more difficult later on to separate. Separations create opportunities for you to empower yourself, to see you can survive without them.

If you do consider reconciliation, a track record needs to be established before you can know a former abuser is safe to be around. And only if there's been a consistent ability to control their anger for at least six months would I recommend going to therapy with them to begin reconciliation efforts. Any individual therapy the abuser is attending should be focused on anger management and self-regulation, where they are learning skills to practice walking away and self-soothing, not just managing anxiety, depression, or addictions, for these are symptoms of greater underlying issues. Dialectical Behavioral Therapy (DBT) is specifically focused on teaching individuals how to tolerate and manage intense emotions. And because we know history always has an outcome, I also recommend a therapy that explores the roots of learned behavior and the person's family-of-origin experiences.

You will likely need the help of a therapist to do these things, and also the support of friends and family. When you are in the cycle of abuse, it can be disorienting and hard to know if you are doing the right thing because you have likely been gaslit and told you are the problem. If people have expressed concerns for you, take that seriously. You are not alone. There are domestic violence shelters that offer places to stay, support groups, educational groups, and free or low-cost legal advice. Many others have broken the cycle of abuse, and you can too!

For Controllers

I know someone hurt you—a parent or an adult who was supposed to be a trusted person, or a childhood bully. That was not fair, or right. You likely had a difficult childhood, and I have great compassion for that. What you endured, and not being able to escape, or not having the experiences of loving connection, has robbed you of the lessons you needed to create secure attachments. I know it can be hard to even admit you have been abusive or controlling. That is the power of shame. You likely got shameful and humiliating messages for showing vulnerability in childhood. And those beliefs are still driving your life today.

Your control is driven by fear, whether you are willing to admit that or not. A fear that others won't want you. That's why you try and control them to stay with you. You were taught a false version of power in relationships—control over others—rather than a power to create positive outcomes for yourself from self-control. When you learn this, people will choose to stay with you out of free will. Free will is needed for love, and people can't choose to stay with you if they don't believe they can leave.

True respect is not gained from fear; it is gained from love. And true power is being able to tame your emotions.

Come join me in recovery and discover how love should be. You'll finally find freedom by letting go of your control.

In the next chapter we'll look at what a secure attachment involves, and the action steps to create it.

REFLECT

1. Growing up, did you have a parent who was abusive, dangerous, chaotic, controlling, victim-like, or neglectful? If so, what impact do you think this had on your attachment to them and on your ability to trust others as safe, consistent, and reliable to meet your needs in your adult relationships?

2. Is your spouse a Controller? Are you fearful of them? If so, what steps do you need to take to get to safety and what boundaries do you need to set to find balance in your relationship?

3. Is your spouse a Victim? If so, and you are a Controller, are you willing to go through an anger management program, individual therapy, addiction recovery, and/or a structured therapeutic separation while financially supporting them until you can be safe? If you are not a Controller, what can you do to encourage your spouse to develop an adult voice and move to becoming an empowered survivor?

4. Do you have a friend or family member who has tendencies of a Controller or Victim attachment style? While maintaining appropriate boundaries, how can you show compassion for them, understanding their childhood was dangerous or chaotic and they need time and effort to grow beyond those experiences?

5. Are you an adoptive or foster parent of a child who came from a chaotic home? If so, do you know their specific experiences of abuse, neglect, or extreme inconsistency from a caregiver that might fuel their fear that their needs can't be met by you? What do you think you can do to help them feel safe? What support do you need, knowing that it will take time for them to trust and learn how to be in a safe relationship with you?

Chapter Nine

Security Is Still Possible— The Secure Connector

Not too long ago I went to a large shopping mall. You know the ones that have several entrances that all look the same, and once inside, you feel like a rat in a maze? I went to the mall map near where I parked, and was glad to find it helpfully color-coded, with stores alphabetized and corresponding lot numbers. It didn't take me long to find the store I wanted. The only problem was there was no "You Are Here" indicated!

Secure attachment is the destination everyone wants, but our journey to get there is different depending on where we start. By now, your attachment injuries and how they formed may be clear, but we don't learn how to do something as foreign as relating securely without seeing how to do it. Many of us can identify behaviors in our parents that were dysfunctional and vow not to commit the same mistakes. However, if you only see a wrong way to solve a math problem, knowing it's wrong doesn't mean you know how to get to the solution. Once you learn how to solve the problem, then it's easy to see where you went wrong and the steps to get there. Only when you can see your current attachment from the starting place of secure attachment will you *fully* know how to solve the insecure pattern you're stuck in.

Remember Lauren's husband from Chapter 5, who took time to ask their children how they were feeling when they were hurt or scared? He learned secure attachment in childhood, so exploring emotions felt natural to him. Imagine that! Or remember Kevin from Chapter 4, who was able to give a more secure response to his girlfriend by looking underneath his anger? He was earning secure attachment by seeing his reactivity and noticing his true feelings of being abandoned in the past. These are the only two ways emotional security can be found in life; we either learn it in childhood as our initial programming or must earn it in adulthood by reprogramming. Now, earning secure attachment means us doing internal reconditioning work, not in the sense of needing to learn how to earn someone's love, but as in the wise words of Yoda, "you must unlearn what you have learned."*

> Earning secure attachment means us doing internal reconditioning work.

The characteristics of secure attachment represent the ideal, but don't expect anyone to exhibit all of these all the time. Having a secure attachment does not mean you are and feel perfectly secure. It means you have developed the observing self to identify triggers to strong emotions and can *more often than not* overcome your reactive impulses to give a more adaptive response that drives connection with others. It also means that when you do react, you recover quickly and take responsibility, apologize, and make a commitment along with an accountable plan to self-correct.

The Securely Attached Child's Experience

Picture two small children making sandcastles near the water's edge at a crowded beach. As their parents watch them from beach chairs, a big wave crashes and knocks them to the wet sand. They scramble to stand up again as the water recedes, clearly surprised by the wave's

---

* *The Empire Strikes Back*, directed by Irvin Kershner (1980).

strength. The father of one child notices his child's distress and comes to help rinse him off, asking if he's okay. The mother of the other child, unmoved, simply shouts toward her son, "When you're playing that close, that's what is going to happen!"

Now, maybe the mother can tell her child isn't physically hurt, and might think getting knocked down is a good life lesson for building awareness and toughness. But the mother doesn't know how that experience felt to her child, and only when a child feels securely attached (seen, known, loved, and understood) can getting knocked down by a wave be a potentially positive *relational* life lesson because they know they have a soothing parent they can go to if the stress gets too much. Without a parent or caring adult attuned to their emotional state, children do not learn they're safe enough to withstand life's surprises.

The securely attached parent is attuned to their child. They can interpret the child's emotions and needs from observing their behaviors and inquiring about their experiences. They teach the child language for emotions, model empathy and validate their experiences, and help the child make connections to corresponding needs so they learn how themselves and become confident to ask for them. This parent is patient and able to manage their own emotions, which models for the child that this is the desired behavior for relationships and that this expectation can be achieved. The child also comes to accept the limits the parent provides are there to protect them, as the parent discusses them openly, allowing natural consequences when necessary. The child feels safe with the parent's calm demeanor, soothing comfort, and predictability of nurturing responses.

As they grow, a secure child feels encouraged and empowered to take age-appropriate risks, trying out for things, and exploring different activities to see how they like them. They know their value is not in how they perform because they know their parent's love is based on who they are to them, not what they do. The child learns to recognize their strengths as their parent affirms them, and they naturally learn their limitations and areas to improve in from genuine, constructive, and supportive feedback. They're encouraged to form their own perspectives, and the parent listens to their ideas. When they need perspective, the parent helps but allows them to figure out what's best by inviting thought, posing questions and providing other perspectives for the child to consider.

> They know their parent's love is based on who they are, not what they do.

Because the child's opinions are welcomed, they learn to appreciate others' thoughtful opinions, even when there are differences in perspectives. And because they're encouraged to take risks, when mistakes occur, the child learns from them and is given opportunities, when possible, to try again. Offering the child forgiveness, and giving apologies that are sincere and caring, teaches the child to also forgive and take responsibility. And the child learns from the parent's behavior how to share, take turns, and wait patiently.

With a loving, consistent caregiver as a secure base the child can return to for help and reassurance, this child becomes a securely attached adult who can:

- Identify emotions driving behaviors with language for them
- Understand *corresponding needs* those emotions indicate, and has confidence in requesting them
- Recognize emotions and needs of others, and respond with empathy
- Self-soothe when needs do not get met
- Exercise self-control to wait patiently for things they want
- Take responsibility for obligations, and accountability for mistakes
- Apologize with humility for mistakes
- Tolerate and stay engaged discussing perspectives they don't hold or agree with
- Set and hold healthy boundaries with others

Attraction and Bonding

The securely attached adult attracts both secure and insecure people. However, they watch for how others recognize and verbalize emotions, request for their needs, self-soothe, and recover from hurts. While those with insecure attachments expect others to pick up on their self-protective strategies and adapt to their insecurities, the Secure Connector quickly picks up on insecure behaviors from others and sets healthy boundaries. Others in relationships with the Secure Connector either become more secure, as they respect and adjust to these boundaries, or they find themselves eventually no longer closely connected, as the Secure Connector is comfortable distancing and detaching when relationships are not reciprocal or emotionally healthy. The Secure Connector's relational awareness drives them to only seek deep relationships with other securely attached individuals or those making efforts to earn secure attachment. These things hold true for all the Secure Connector's adult relationships (friends, family, and romantic partners).

> The Secure Connector quickly picks up on insecure behaviors from others and sets healthy boundaries.

What Secure Relationships Are

Securely attached relationships are where each person can negotiate, compromise, take turns, share, and coregulate:

Negotiate—We hear each other out and thoughtfully consider before making decisions that affect one another.
Compromise—We both get some of what we want.
Take turns—We alternate who chooses so both people's likes are explored and appreciated.
Share—We each take part and own our part.
Coregulate—We comfort one another.

To do these things, Secure Connectors must be flexible, be able to self-regulate, have impulse control, be able to wait their turn, and listen and communicate well. And by being aware of emotions, both theirs and others', they can manage stress, validate other's perspectives, empathize, have realistic expectations, and be able to offer grace and forgiveness.

Early Lessons

Now, you may not have had a secure parent who taught you the lessons the secure child learns, or known what a securely attached relationship truly looked like as you got into adulthood, but many of these social-emotional lessons are also introduced early at school. The lessons likely didn't stick if they weren't reinforced or modeled appropriately in your home. See if some of these sound familiar from Kindergarten:

- Recognizing and labeling emotions of fictional characters during story time
- Asking and waiting to speak when you wanted something by raising your hand in the air
- Recognizing others' needs to use the bathroom first
- Waiting and taking turns on the playground
- Controlling your impulses and delaying gratification when you had to wait for your snack
- Sharing toys in the classroom and cooperating with the teacher
- Asking for help from the teacher and problem-solving on your work
- Taking responsibility and doing your share during clean-up time
- Apologizing when you hurt others
- Listening to others during show-and-tell
- Being flexible when schedules didn't go to plan, like the school bus being delayed for the field trip

- Accepting disappointment when you couldn't play outside because it was raining
- Forgiving and giving grace when a classmate was having a difficult day

Though these may have seemed simple ideas at the time, learning to get along with others in the classroom from an early age was important to our long-term development. And collectively, with consistent reinforcement in all environments, these lessons form vital stages that should have allowed us the ability to graduate into healthy, secure adults.

If we take a moment to view what having learned these lessons looks like in adulthood, they can help define how secure adults act.

Recognizing and Labeling Emotions

We understand our behaviors are often rooted in deeper emotions, and that when we feel something difficult—like sadness or fear—it's usually pointing to an unmet need. We're then able to soften our anger and look beneath it, recognizing the more tender emotions it might be protecting, like hurt or vulnerability. With this self-awareness, we can share our feelings in a way that invites empathy and builds meaningful connection. Instead of pushing discomfort away, we give ourselves permission to feel our emotions. By tuning into how emotions show up in our body, we develop an inner early-warning system, which helps us care for our feelings before they become overwhelming.

Asking When We Want Something

We know that others can't read our mind, so we communicate our needs with kind and clear requests. When we speak in a way that invites connection and understanding, it makes it more likely our needs will be met. When someone says no, we take a moment to reflect on whether the request was reasonable. If it was, we hold space for our disappointment while recognizing the other person's hesitation may come from their own fears or limitations. And if the refusal feels unfair, we're able to navigate the rejection without losing confidence in ourselves or our right to ask for what we need from others in the future.

Recognizing Others' Needs and Helping Them

We notice when others need support but don't rush in to take over. We allow others to try on their own when they're able, and step in only when help is truly needed. We offer support—either when asked or when someone is clearly struggling—and only in a way that empowers or builds partnership, not control or codependency. By asking "What do you need?" in a caring way, we can help others feel safe and encourage them to ask for help when they need it.

Waiting and Taking Turns

We patiently wait our turn, understanding that others who struggle with waiting may still be working on their emotional maturity. We stand firm when necessary, but we don't let feelings of unfairness provoke a reaction when others act out of turn. We understand other people's reactions often stem from their own unresolved issues.

Controlling Our Impulses and Delaying Gratification

We can pause and redirect our focus when something isn't beneficial in the moment. We consider the long-term impact of our actions, to exercise self-control and choose what's best for the bigger picture. While we acknowledge our feelings as a sign of our needs, we understand they are temporary and don't always define what's true or necessary in the moment. Therefore, we rely on our objective guides—our values, spiritual beliefs, or personal standards—to assess if our emotions are disproportionate or misplaced. This helps us remember how our choices might affect others, because we believe what's best for everyone, not just ourselves, is usually the right course of action.

> While we acknowledge our feelings as a sign of our needs, we understand they are temporary and don't always define what's true or necessary in the moment.

Sharing and Cooperating

Balancing what we want and need with others is important, especially when we both want to do something different and only one way can be chosen. When a resource is limited, we can negotiate fair solutions, even if it means not getting everything we want. We're comfortable allowing others to have a turn or at times have something if they need it more. At the same time, we ensure resources are shared to meet our needs too, setting boundaries to model self-respect and maintain healthy relationships.

Asking for Help with Problem-Solving

When we've reached our limit and need help, we can ask for it. We don't look to others to solve problems for us, but know help can empower us to learn more effectively and stay humble. We try to understand how we arrived at the problem, and we remember what we learn from this so we can avoid getting stuck in the same area again in the future.

Taking Responsibility

People can trust us because we take charge of our responsibilities and follow through. We do our work and let others do theirs, but we understand things can't always be divided perfectly and everyone has different abilities. We don't leave things undone that would affect a third party just because someone else can't or won't help, though we work to ensure things are fair and say no when others try to take advantage. We can resist pressure from others, even if they show displeasure toward us, because we understand that real love includes limits, and that healthy boundaries create security for everyone. This encourages others to commit to doing their part.

Apologizing When We Hurt Others

We take responsibility for mistakes, even unintentional ones. We're humble and confident enough to apologize, accept the consequences, and make amends. At the same time, we don't take responsibility for things that aren't our fault or over-apologize out of fear. When someone feels hurt by something we don't believe was wrong, we stay open, knowing that listening with care to understand someone's feelings doesn't mean taking the blame.

Listening to Others

We can respect others' perspectives while maintaining our own so we can listen and truly understand their concerns. We can wait our turn to speak without interrupting or correcting people, even when we don't agree. If someone becomes hurtful or aggressive, we are confident creating space until the conversation can continue in a safe and respectful way. And we can think of thoughtful and relevant questions to ask to increase our understanding and help the other person feel heard. When others give us constructive feedback, we consider it thoughtfully and without defensiveness or shame. We do these things not out of fear, but to model how we expect others to listen to us.

Being Flexible

We hold firm to our values and healthy boundaries, yet remain open to new information and adjust to changes. We recognize that problems often have several solutions and can thoughtfully consider what the best option may be. If others want different things, we can compromise. And we make decisions carefully to avoid second-guessing ourselves, so once we've made the choice, we commit to it.

Accepting Disappointment

We can accept what we can't change, even when we don't like it or agree. We can quickly move past hurts and disappointments to focus on moving forward and learning from the experience. We understand that avoiding disappointment is not the goal in life, and that growth often occurs through challenging moments. Our primary goal in life isn't to always feel happy, but to live in a healthy and grounded way, because this is what's most beneficial for us.

Forgiving and Giving Grace

We believe disagreement can be a sign of trust when it's done in a space where differences can be expressed openly with emotional safety. We also know disagreement can help reveal blind spots to support our growth, so we disagree without being disagreeable or rude. When we are hurt by others, we forgive and show grace, because we know we also need it. And we don't hold grudges because we know holding on to resentment causes more harm than healing—for both parties. We know forgiveness often produces greater security and a feeling of safety in relationships.

Communicating in Conflict

The Secure Connector's communication is:

- **Clear**—Their message is straightforward, leaving no confusion about the direction of the conversation.
- **Coherent**—Their reasoning is structured in a way that is easy to follow and understand.
- **Concise**—They succinctly state what they mean and don't use more words than necessary or repeat themselves.
- **Collaborative**—They communicate in way that encourages connection while seeking to listen as much as they speak.

Communicating this way makes it easier for others to understand and reduces confusion.

The Secure Connector knows navigating conflict involves taking time to listen, exploring others' feelings, and side-stepping criticism, and that they don't need to defend against every accusation. When the other person focuses on perceived faults, Secure Connectors redirect them to focus on their emotional needs to help them share without blaming.

Helping another person identify feelings allows Secure Connectors to empathize with that person's emotional experience even when they don't agree with their perspective. Secure Connectors try to find common ground, whether by acknowledging part of the other person's perspective they *can* agree with, or by identifying an outcome they both want, to find a mutual resolution. Having modeled what effective listening looks like, they then can ask if others will listen to them in the same attentive, respectful, and empathetic way.

When it is their turn to speak, Secure Connectors use "I" statements to describe their feelings and experiences in subjective ways. "I feel _____," or "I would like if _____." This helps others acknowledge the Secure Connector's feelings without feeling blamed. They also demonstrate ownership for managing their own negative emotions, rather than blaming others for how they feel or expecting someone to change as the only way for them to recover. These skills enable Secure Connectors to achieve the deep closeness that comes from relational repair. While not all conflicts result in mutual understanding, Secure Connectors do their part to nurture the relationship and invite others into mature communication.

Self-Soothing

Healthy internal dialogue is essential for learning to soothe in moments of stress. Secure Connectors can talk themselves through emotional flooding to stay calm and find relief. They see beneath anger and anxiety to focus on the underlying, primary emotions—sadness, hurt, shame, or fear. And they use their observing self to recognize triggers when their emotional reactions are out of proportion to the present situation. This enables them to recognize defensiveness and tolerate negative feelings, knowing intense emotions are not always solely caused by the present situation.

Growth

Secure Connectors take ownership of their growth and recognize that discipline, effort, and continuous improvement are essential for building healthy relationships. Having developed insight and self-awareness, Secure Connectors identify their growth goals and intentionally practice them regularly. By holding themselves accountable, they reduce the need for others to do so or point out their flaws. They also know that growth is a lifelong process, which reduces unrealistic expectations about how quickly they, or others, should be growing.

Earning Secure Attachment (for Adults)

Secure Connectors are aware of and honest about their flaws, and committed to doing something about them. As you learn to be more secure, you will also need a secure base in a mentor, therapist, partner, or friend to help support your insight and awareness, empathize and validate your experiences, give comfort, and model secure strategies. Secure attachment can only be learned in the process of another person showing you how to attach securely with them.

I know becoming secure sounds like a lot of work! When I first started, I was both in awe that a person could respond this way yet also disheartened because I knew I was far from being like this. But by being faithful to the process of growth, I have inched my way closer to security month by month, and year by year, so that now, I am far more hopeful and able to model more of these skills. This is why I know it works, and that you can do it too!

"How long will this take?" is a question I often hear at the beginning of therapy. Your specific timeline depends on how many of these questions you can genuinely answer with a "yes":

- Are you disciplined?
- Can you wait your turn?
- Can you listen for understanding when you don't have agreement?
- Can you control your impulsivity and reactivity?
- Can you communicate your needs and desires clearly and effectively?
- Can you recover from mistakes quickly?
- Can you admit wrongdoing and apologize sincerely?

These questions are likely correlated to what was modeled for you growing up. And your answers reflect what work you have already done to recognize these as areas of growth. While growth can feel overwhelming and discouraging at times, it comes with a clear reward. As you learn and develop, you'll progress through the *four stages of competence*, a process that reflects your effort and increased understanding. And if you can keep going—even when it's hard—knowing the journey is worth it, you will progress into competence:

> Can you communicate your needs and desires clearly and effectively?

Stage 1. Unconscious Incompetence is when we are unaware of what we are doing wrong. No insight or awareness has happened yet. Like the *Titanic*, heading directly for the iceberg and unaware of the catastrophe about to unfold, we're like the *Titanic*'s radio operators who received at least six warnings of ice and icebergs but disregarded them all.

Stage 2. Conscious Incompetence occurs when we become aware of what we are doing wrong, but haven't yet made a change or are unable to stop our reactions. This is when you can see more than just the tip of the iceberg. You are now faced with the giant mass underneath and all the practice work ahead. Some people get stuck in this stage, overwhelmed by shame or by the amount of effort required for transformation.

Stage 3. Conscious Competence is when we're actively working to do the right thing with our practice work. With consistent effort, we succeed at times and fail at others, but we pick ourselves up and continue trying to break the pattern.

Stage 4. Unconscious Competence is reached when our practice has become habit. You will know you've arrived at this stage when you no longer have to think about how to respond to relational stress appropriately. You know what to do because you've practiced it. You still have lifelong work to do, but you've earned secure attachment through the reward of all your efforts, and it is now your new default way of bonding.

All of this is achievable and not as complicated as it may seem at first. With the right practices, everything is just a matter of time and effort. Now you've gained some insight and are becoming more aware, let's move on to Step Three and get clear on what best practices you can begin employing to achieve secure attachment.

> **REFLECT**
>
> 1. Which characteristics of the Secure Connector stood out as surprising or especially noteworthy?
>
> 2. Were you able to recognize anyone you know in some of the description, or did it sound like an ideal persona that's not truly achievable?
>
> 3. Which of these lessons did you learn growing up? Who taught them to you?
>
> 4. Which of these lessons have you learned in adulthood? Who taught them to you? Can that person serve as a secure base for continued growth?
>
> 5. Which of these lessons do you still need to learn? Are there specific ones you're more eager or ready to begin with?

Step Three

Show Up to Practice

> Knowledge is of no value unless you put it into practice.
>
> Attributed to Anton Chekhov

I'm hoping by now you've become more aware of everyday minor instances that might be rekindling old neural networks of danger from somewhere in your deep history where a need went unmet.

Maybe you're beginning to notice that it does bother you more than it should when you have to wait on someone, even when it's only for a few seconds or minutes.

Or, you're realizing there might be a reason why you're so uncomfortable when someone cries in front of you, even when you're not the cause.

Or, you're now noticing the anxiety you have over even small decisions, such as where to pick to eat, is because you worry someone is going to be disappointed.

Congratulations! That's your observing self!

And if you've identified some specific emotional triggers and made a few links to the historical events where some of your wounds occurred, you're beginning to form an outline for your coherent narrative of how your upbringing has shaped your adult attachment style.

The growth goals that follow will help you build new neural pathways, but like exercising muscles, consistent practice is the only way to build resilience and competence. I can't overstate the importance of this. Practicing your specific goals is how you earn secure attachment.

> Practicing your specific goals is how you earn secure attachment.

Our modern Western culture conditions us to resist discomfort. Food and almost any product can be delivered directly to our homes. We can place orders on our phones and have a pick-up time, so we don't have to wait in line, with some businesses even meeting us at the car with the purchase. Entertainment is streamed on demand, and we can "binge watch" entire seasons of a show in a single day.

I admit, I do not enjoy waiting (part of recovering from my insecure attachment style), and I appreciate all the features and benefits of modern-day Western living. But as you will discover in this next section, insight and awareness are only the beginnings of growth. Unfortunately, there's no replacement or shortcut for the existential and practical efforts of doing an action repeatedly to acquire the skills for transformation. Growth requires exercising in the "Earned Security" gym.

As you begin building tolerance for negative emotions, these practices will help you notice your reactivity and start responding in more constructive ways. And in time, these new skills will move to the category of unconscious competence, where they become your default way of appropriately managing stress and securely relating to others.

Some of it may be difficult, but remember: The choice is either the short-term discomfort of growth in seeking after wholeness, or the longer-term pain of staying wounded and continuing to be insecurely attached. It's painful either way, but only one path leads to freedom.

Chapter Ten

Growth Goals

The growth journey for your best friend, or your neighbor, or your parent, is unique to them, just as yours is to you. You can't do their work, but you *can* do your own. This is where the steps of developing insight and becoming aware get applied and have the potential to produce real change, as you can take practical steps to grow into the emotionally healthy person you were designed to be.

Which attachment style resonated most with you? In which one did you recognize parts of yourself? Spend time with the following growth goals, focusing on the attachment areas where you feel most challenged.

Avoider Growth Goals

Here's how to begin growing from your dismissive-avoidant insecure attachment:

Develop the Observing Self Begin to notice your tendency to disconnect from your emotions, avoid deeper connection, and blame others for relationship problems. These habits prevent self-reflection. When you acknowledge these self-protective strategies and learn to linger and reflect on what is actually going on inside you, you will begin to engage your observing self. This will help you take responsibility for how your role of avoidance *equally* contributes to negative cycles.

See Avoidance as a Developmental Injury If you tend to avoid emotions, you might see it as strength, priding yourself on independence and staying in control. But if you examine your history, you'll see that your emotional distancing isn't how you were born; it was something you learned. No baby enters this world without a deep need for emotional connection, especially with their mother. Shutting down became a way to protect yourself when no one was there to help you make sense of your feelings. If you struggle to handle emotions, your own or others', that's not a flaw. It's an emotional injury, and a stage of development that was missed. What once helped you cope is keeping you from growing into the emotionally connected adult you're meant to be. The good news is, it's not too late to grow! By acknowledging where your emotional growth was interrupted, you can begin the work of healing and step into a fuller, more connected version of yourself.

Develop Emotional Intelligence Avoiders often respond with "I'm fine" because they struggle to identify what they're truly feeling. But emotional intelligence—understanding how emotions shape behavior and signal needs—is paramount for healthy relationships. When you can name your emotions, you're better able to ask for support and understand what others might need from you, too. Learning to speak the language of emotion helps you express your inner world and connect more deeply with others. Instead of pushing feelings aside or focusing only on what seems "logical," try tuning in with the help of a list of emotions and then share how you feel. You might be surprised how much your relationships grow and how helpful feelings actually are!

Connect Mind and Body Emotions are also feelings experienced in the body. Avoiders are often unaware of the impact of emotions on the body because they suppress them. When we express emotions, we release that physical tension, but when we suppress them it stays stored inside. If you allow your emotions to surface you will see it not only brings relief but also builds empathy for what others feel. Mindfulness practices that connect body and mind can help activate parts of the brain that didn't fully develop due to limited emotional connection in early relationships. With practice, this connection can grow, and so can your capacity to feel, relate, and heal.

Let Others In Avoiders often try to handle challenges on their own because it feels "weak" to ask for help or you don't expect anyone will be willing or available. But when you're going through something hard, don't carry it alone. Letting others support you gives them a meaningful place in your life. It also creates space for connection, shared strength, and the kind of community we're all wired to need and enjoy. When you can do this you will find a whole new side to relationships you've been missing out on.

> Letting others support you gives them a meaningful place in your life.

Be Vulnerable Do you cringe at this phrase? Many Avoiders quickly pull back from emotional moments. They might look away, laugh, change the subject, or make a joke when faced with their own or someone else's pain. These habits—developed as protection—create walls that not only keep others out but also keep you locked in, unable to reach out for connection. When we can look into each other's eyes, it makes the connection more personal because it reveals our internal states. Vulnerability is the only way to see more and be seen more, and that's how real connection grows.

Give your loved ones permission to let you know you're doing these avoidant practices to recondition yourself, and share how you're trying to overcome your own resistance. Allowing yourself to be vulnerable will make a big difference in the depth of your relationships.

Prioritize Connection over Production Avoiders are often admired for their strong work ethic and dedication. But when so much attention is placed on productivity—either your own or pushing others to meet high standards—it can take time and energy away from truly connecting on a human level. When people feel like they're valued more for what they do than who they are, it can create resistance or even lead to rebellion. While holding others accountable is important, it needs to be rooted in a relationship built on trust and care. You can be a high achiever and still be tender with people. In the end, it's not the chores or accomplishments we remember most; it's the people we shared life with. Don't be one who wishes they put more effort into building relationships than they did at getting ahead at work. Take time to truly know and enjoy your loved ones. They may not always be there.

Listen, Don't Fix Deflecting negative emotions by minimizing, dismissing, telling jokes, and problem-solving tries to change a person's feelings. Accept your discomfort and know "cheering up" is not what people need unless they ask for it. When someone is hurting or in distress, what they need is to feel *seen*, *heard*, and *understood*.

Listening is not passive; it's recognizing the emotions expressed and actively engaging in the speaker's experience by asking relevant questions to learn more. It's repeating back what they said so you and they know you heard and understood them. It's leaning in, nodding to affirm, and making empathetic, validating gestures and statements. And when you don't know what someone wants, it's asking them how you can help. Good listening is attentive, active, and reflective.

Seek Connection Typical complaints about Avoiders are that they seem content to not go deep or seek connection. When connection only goes one way, it's easy to see who's putting in the effort. Loved ones grow tired of this, and when their relationships start to break down,

Avoiders are then thrust into making substantial efforts to pursue the other person if they want to save the relationship.

Being proactive in initiating engagement will help balance your relationships. Reciprocate with others' requests by inviting them to spend time with you and doing things with them that they enjoy. Show affection, and say how you feel: "I enjoy being with you," "Your friendship means a lot to me," and "I love you." Sharing your emotions, and telling others how they can help you, will become more natural as you grow.

Pleaser Growth Goals

Here are ways to begin growing out of your anxious-permissive insecure style:

Develop the Observing Self Pleasers are usually so focused on how others are feeling and reacting that they abandon themselves by minimizing their needs, pacifying others, or tolerating disrespect. Work on becoming aware of when you do this and consider your *own* emotions that are being triggered. It's because you continually give in to appease others that your relationships remain stuck.

Becoming aware of these self-protective strategies will help you see that appeasing others does not make your relational problems go away for long, and will challenge you to change your part in the giver-taker dynamic.

Recognize Your Anxiety Pleasers often take on the "helper" role, but it's more to ease their own anxiety at seeing others in need than it is to help. Helping also ensures they are needed by others, which unconsciously serves to protect them against potential future abandonment. Some Pleasers don't recognize they're driven by anxiety. They've lived with it for so many years that it's become their baseline functioning feeling.

If your acts of "love," overprotection, pleasing, and appeasing are driven by your fears, then those are self-serving. Only once you acknowledge your anxiety can you do something about it and get on the path to healing. True healing begins when you can name your anxiety as your part in dysfunctional relational patterns. Learning to manage anxiety is the way to become less anxious, not ignoring it, distracting from it, or reacting to control outcomes.

Address Problems Pleasers are not good at sitting in the tension that is needed for relational growth to occur. They avoid conflict by minimizing, being indirect, or not being honest about their true feelings or desires to keep the peace. The only way to get better at confronting is to practice it! You can be kind, yet honest at the same time. Focusing on the issue rather than the person helps keep the conversation objective and prevents unnecessary hurt feelings. Avoid handling disagreement through text, email, or leaving notes behind—these can make honest responses less likely and hinder your tolerance building for confrontation.

> The only way to get better at confronting is to practice it.

Each time you set and hold a boundary, you grow stronger. With practice, your anxiety around confrontation will ease. And, over time, others will be less likely to push past your limits, leading to more respectful relationships and a reduced need to confront. Confidence comes with doing, and you'll see that you're more capable than you think.

Stand Up to Destructive Anger Anger and frustration are natural and can be valid, but should be expressed respectfully. There are times when Pleasers allow others to speak harshly or act meanly without saying anything. This does not foster mutual respect. Instead of freezing or rushing to smooth things over, it's important to speak up and calmly confront disrespectful behavior. Being kind and easygoing shouldn't mean tolerating mistreatment. Respect is not always earned either;

sometimes it needs to be commanded by standing your ground. You can be both gracious and firm. The two can go hand in hand.

Discover Your Anger Pleasers are often afraid of other people's anger, so they tend to suppress their own. But feeling anger isn't wrong; it's natural, and it has a purpose to motivate us to action. Anger can be a powerful force for protection and change when expressed in healthy ways. When used to defend yourself or others, anger can be constructive. It only becomes destructive when it's used to hurt someone or when it's turned inward. Learning to feel and express anger appropriately allows you to stand up for yourself and channel the adrenaline that anxiety creates into courage to set and hold boundaries.

It's adaptive to have both a "stand your ground" and a "fight to protect" response. Sometimes, a firm response is exactly what's needed for others to take you seriously and back down. Learning to feel and use anger appropriately is key for a Pleaser's growth.

Endure Displeasure Pleasers often fawn or try to quickly smooth things over when someone is upset with them. They also are often overcommitted because they have a hard time saying no to requests. But it will be okay when others are unhappy with you simply for holding healthy boundaries. Discomfort, disappointment, and even displeasure are part of life—and not all conflict is bad. Sometimes conflict is the means for others to see they can't always get what they want.

True intimacy isn't possible without learning how to navigate conflict. When you never disagree or speak up for yourself, your relationships remain shallow, because the other person doesn't have to consider your needs. Sometimes, the best gift you can give is space for others to calm down, reflect, and grow. If you rush in to fix things too quickly, you may rob both yourself and the other person of important growth to develop resilience and deeper understanding.

Make Decisions Pleasers are often seen as easygoing, but allowing others to choose isn't always about kindness. You may believe you're deferring to others because you enjoy seeing them happy, but deep down, it's often because you're anxious about conflict or them being disappointed or upset at you. If you were conditioned in childhood to give in, you may not have had the chance to develop decision-making skills, or even have got to know your own preferences.

You can start discovering what you like by simply making more choices, even if you're unsure at first. That's how clarity comes. And remember: It's okay if others feel disappointed sometimes. Taking turns is a healthy part of any relationship. When the other person always gets what they want, it's not beneficial for you or them. When you start asserting your needs and making decisions, you're practicing self-respect. This will not only help reduce your anxiety but also build real confidence in yourself.

Don't Rescue If it feels unbearable to watch someone struggle, that's often a sign of your own growth area. When Pleasers step in to rescue too quickly, they may unintentionally take away someone's chance to grow. Fixing problems for others before they've had a chance to try, fail, and learn can keep them dependent and create a cycle of codependency. You can't empower someone if you do it for them. True support means walking beside them, not in front of them, as they find their own strength.

Accept Help Pleasers are often quick to notice and care for the needs of others, yet they tend to downplay or ignore their own, often apologizing when others see them struggling and jump in to help. Much of their giving is driven by a desire for acceptance or to be needed, which can make receiving help feel undeserved or uncomfortable because it rebalances the relationship.

Though it may feel uncomfortable at first, allowing others to support you is a gift to them, too. It gives them the chance to use and develop their strengths. You are not a burden. Letting others care for you creates connection, and honors the way we're all designed to give and receive love. It also allows your relationships to be balanced so you don't get burned out.

Find Comfort Being Alone Introverted Pleasers may enjoy solitude as a way to soothe their anxiety, but Extroverted Pleasers may struggle with being alone because their sense of identity is so closely tied to their relationships. Extroverted Pleasers often stay busy and surround themselves with people to avoid being alone, so when someone wants space, it can feel like rejection or even abandonment.

But learning who you are on your own—as a "me"—is just as important as knowing who you are in a relationship—as a "we." Rather than planning your day around others or filling your time to busy yourself when you can't, try leaning into moments of solitude. You might be surprised by what you discover about yourself.

Learn the Power of Confident Body Language Anxiety often shows up in our body language—like bouncing legs, fidgeting, slouched shoulders, looking down, or avoiding eye contact. These signals can unintentionally communicate a lack of confidence, which may make others more likely to take advantage of Pleasers.

Practicing confident posture will help you have mental confidence. Start by breathing deeply and opening your chest to straighten your shoulders. Stand tall or sit upright. When talking with someone, lean in slightly and relax your arms—elbows out, palms up. When sitting, spread out a little to take up the room in your seat. Maintain steady eye contact, and make gestures with your hands when speaking.

Speak clearly and at a moderate pace, keeping your tone even to avoid ending sentences with an upward pitch that can sound like you are unsure or asking a question. This will help you sound more decisive. Take initiative by making suggestions or making a decision when you're with others. Point in the direction where you want everyone to go when in a group. Hold up your hand like a stop sign when you want someone to stop or not come any closer. When you look and act confident, you'll start to feel it on the inside.

Vacillator Growth Goals

These are the ways to grow out of your anxious-preoccupied ambivalence:

Develop the Observing Self Growing up watching and waiting for a parent to give them time and attention, Vacillators continue in adulthood being overly focused on the actions of others, to see if others are willing to connect with them in *their* desired way. However, this outward focus makes it difficult for them to recognize their own emotional reactions, which often fuel conflict cycles. Blaming and defending keep the focus on others and prevent them from honestly examining their contributions to a problem.

Developing the "observing self" is the way to gain self-awareness, which will help you take responsibility for your triggers so you can learn to be less reactive. This is where real growth—and deeper connection—will begin for you.

Own Your Triggers (MUDWARS) Vacillators are triggered when they feel **m**isunderstood, feel **u**nseen or unheard, get **d**isappointed over failed idealized outcomes, are made to **w**ait (especially for time and attention), perceive **a**bandonment or **r**ejection, or feel **s**hame over their bad behaviors or not feeling good enough for others. These feelings, along with your anger and hopelessness, began in childhood but continue to haunt you today by coloring your interactions in the present. Recognize others are inadvertently triggering your old childhood wounds, rather than being the cause of all your pain in the present.

Empathize with your younger self who was either abandoned or unseen, and realize that these are core wounds from childhood hurts which you are still acutely sensitive to. While your feelings are real, your reactivity toward others can subside as you learn to deal with your childhood hurts and keep them from flooding into the present.

Stop the "BADDProDD" Pattern When a "$50 reaction" to a "5-cent problem" happens, notice a core wound was subconsciously triggered. If your emotion is out of proportion to the event, past pain is flooding into the present. Remember your self-protective pattern to **b**lame, get **a**ngry, **d**evalue others, **d**efend your actions, and **pro**test to get others to notice and apologize, and then **d**espairing and **d**etaching if it doesn't work. When you get upset, remember how this pattern began early on as a reaction to the triggers you experienced.

Learn to verbalize rather than dramatize what you feel. Look under your anger and express more vulnerable feelings. Instead of blaming, vie for the empathy you want. As you uncover and voice your past injury, your anger and hopelessness will reduce. The earlier you can recognize where you are in this pattern, the better chance you have of not going through the rest of the reactive steps, and you will heal a little bit each time.

Accept Mistakes Vacillators often label people—including themselves—as "bad" rather than seeing the behavior as the issue. Everyone makes mistakes, and they're often integral to how we learn. Shifting this mindset can ease self-shame as well as reduce harsh judgments toward others.

When you're hurt, use it as an opportunity to practice forgiveness and grace. And when you find yourself stuck in a shame spiral after a mistake or emotional reaction, gently remind yourself: If I can learn from this, I can grow. The more you can label actions—rather than people—the more you'll begin to see others, and yourself, with more compassion. Your tolerance for mistakes will increase, and your resentment, anger, and shame will reduce.

Don't Idealize Vacillators often carry idealistic expectations for how things should go, which makes disappointments feel a lot bigger. Remember that in an imperfect world, some level of disappointment is normal, and not everything will go exactly as hoped. Tell yourself "This may not be as good as I'd like it to be!" when anticipating something, and "This is not as bad as it feels!" when things don't go to plan. Rate situations and emotions in degrees and levels—"okay," "good," "better," "the best," and "not good," "unpleasant," "undesirable." As you learn to manage your idealizations, in turn your disappointments will decrease.

Recognize Rigid Thinking Vacillators can struggle with black-and-white and all-or-nothing thinking, seeing only a "good" or a "bad" option, or that all roads lead to disappointment if they can't get what they want. Learn to be open to other outcomes you may not yet have considered. Accepting differing points of view can help you see there is often more than one result that you can be content with. Remember, two things can be true at once. You can feel sad that your friends didn't choose your favorite restaurant and still have a great time at the place they picked.

When you notice yourself fixating on one "right" outcome, pause and look for the middle ground. You might find more room for flexibility—and contentment—than you expected.

Overcome Ambivalence Vacillators often feel torn between two opposing desires that can keep them stuck, unsure of what they truly want. When feeling this way, the first step is to name what is happening: "I'm feeling ambivalent right now." To move forward, choose one direction, the one that aligns most with your healthiest, most grounded self. It might be the path you'd take if you weren't feeling overwhelmed, worried, fearful, or angry.

Then stop entertaining the other idea. Remind yourself that you are sticking with the choice you've made and that discomfort is expected when we choose growth. As your brain builds this new neural pathway of learning to decide and follow one thing, one idea, one emotion, rather than feeling torn between two or more, the pull of ambivalence will lessen, making decision-making feel clearer and more peaceful.

Shut Down Rumination When Vacillators feel hurt, they often get stuck brooding over it, replaying what happened, what it might have meant, and what could happen next. This is usually set in motion from one or more of their MUDWARS triggers and causes anxiety buildups that often lead to venting to release the anxiety. "Mind reading" (assuming what someone thinks of you) or "fortune-telling" (predicting how someone will treat you) keep you focused on your hurt and not on healing. The way out of rumination is to return to the present. Try these helpful strategies:

- Talk to a trusted friend or pray to process your thoughts.
- Use mindfulness techniques to ground yourself in the moment.
- Distract yourself with something engaging—a podcast, music, show, or game.
- Repeat a comforting scripture, mantra, or prayer to refocus your mind.
- Find a "final thought" from the situation and gently remind yourself of it when your thoughts start to spiral.

With practice, you'll become better at catching yourself entering the spin-cycle and stopping it.

Accept Differentiation of Thoughts Vacillators often over-explain when they feel misunderstood, hoping that being fully seen will create connection. But their zeal to be understood can sometimes do the opposite and create disconnection, because it overshadows their ability to understand others.

People won't always agree, even if they understand your perspective, and that's okay. Show curiosity about others' views and respect their right to think differently. Not all disagreement is rejection, and you might even learn something new that expands your own view. Your strong need to feel understood stems from early wounds. Noticing this can help you respond with more balance. Learning to hold space for both your views and others' is where deeper connection truly begins.

Allow for Individuation of Actions Vacillators may rush into decisions that affect others without consulting them, or pressure others to agree, sometimes using connection as leverage. But when people feel pushed, they often pull away to protect their independence. Respect others' right to do things differently and make their own choices. It's not rejection; it's individuality. Healthy and balanced relationships allow for differences.

Make Requests Vacillators often expect others, especially their partners, to sense their needs without having to ask, and they use this expectation to gauge the strength of the relationship. Because asking creates a risk of rejection, Vacillators tend to pursue with complaints, criticisms, or sulking to get others to pick up on their needs. Instead of hoping others will just "know," try making clear, kind requests. It's a healthier way to get your needs met, and much more likely to lead to connection, rather than conflict.

Notice Anxiety Around Arrivals, Departures, and Waiting Because Vacillators often lacked consistent connection in childhood with at least one important attachment figure, they often experience anxiety around arrivals and departures with others. They tend to have high expectations for arrivals, hoping for deep connection. While departures stir up unconscious abandonment, and waiting creates tension around whether connection will happen at all.

When you feel this anxiety, pause and remind yourself: This feeling has roots in the past, and I'm safe now. Preparing for these moments with awareness can help you stay grounded and respond with calm instead of fear.

Controller Growth Goals

Here are ways Controllers can practice growing out of their authoritarian attachment style:

Develop the Observing Self You learned to fight to survive and keep abuse at bay in childhood, but you are continuing that survival mode in adulthood. This is why you feel constantly on edge. Blaming others for your anger and lashing out is your defense to block deeper, more vulnerable emotions—like fear, insecurity, abandonment, or rejection—that kept you powerless and ashamed in childhood. But as you begin to take responsibility for your agitation and reactions, you can start to see that others aren't trying to anger you, but are triggering old wounds. With awareness comes the power to respond differently.

Understand Why You Control and Let Go Controllers control because unpredictability in childhood meant danger. Your control is driven by fear, so controlling is your way of creating a sense of safety to calm your fears. But not everyone is like the abuser who hurt you. Learning to trust is hard, but possible. Start small: Choose one person you respect, and see if you can let them make a decision that affects you. Bit by bit, you can build trust and feel safe without needing to control others or your environment all the time.

Direct Anger at Your Past The anger from your childhood over what was done to you is real and valid. But to truly heal, that anger needs to be redirected toward the past, not taken out on those around you. Your anger is powerful, and when it's unchecked, it can feel scary for you and for others. Don't be like the abuser in childhood you despised. Seek a therapist and group help and in time you will begin to feel more in control over yourself and your emotions.

Grieve Your Trauma Controllers don't grieve because they often minimize the impact the childhood trauma is having on them in adulthood. Your trauma will continue to affect you, even if you are in denial. You did survive, but it came with a cost. No child should have endured what you did. You made it through because you learned to fight back to stop the suffering. However, you are continuing that fight in adulthood, even though the threats to your survival are gone. This reaction is no longer necessary. When you can admit that you've been traumatized you can get the help you need. Then you will find there is a better way you can learn to express pain without feeling like you need to fight for survival.

Listen to Others and Ask for Their Opinions Controllers don't like to listen; they like to tell. You had someone who did that to you, and you had no choice but to submit. You've vowed never to be in that position again and do the things you hated. But listening to others' opinions now doesn't make you weak; it makes you strong. Hearing someone out and considering their ideas means you can take things in and not feel threatened. If you get angry when others display vulnerability or cry, remember how your tears and vulnerability were not allowed or cared for. If you were ridiculed, you may still not allow yourself to feel vulnerable. But allowing others to have the voice you couldn't is true strength and evidence your abusers have lost control over you.

Replace Intimidation with Mutual Respect For the Controller in childhood, submission meant respect. Anger and intimidation were your model for how a person gets others to do things. When you threaten and intimidate, others may do what you want, but they will despise you for it. There's a different type of respect that is developed through reciprocity—compromising, taking turns, showing dignity, and honoring each other's boundaries. This type of respect is mutual and does not have to be demanded, unlike the type of respect you learned that is gained by fear. As you recognize the difference, you will see that you can have both love *and* respect in a relationship. All healthy relationships do.

Get a Sponsor and a Therapist You can't heal the trauma you endured on your own. You likely need a mentor or sponsor *and* a therapist who can guide and support you as you grow. This will be someone who can give you candid feedback without being intimidated by your anger, yet also who is compassionate to how your past has impacted you. Find someone you respect so you can receive feedback even when it is constructive. Learning to receive empathy and comfort from a safe person who can be directive *and* loving toward you will be key to helping you see that relationships can have both these elements.

Victim Growth Goals

Here are ways Victims can practice growing out of their compliant-helpless attachment style:

Develop the Observing Self Notice how you freeze, comply, and dissociate as a survival mechanism to tolerate the intolerable. In childhood, when no help came, you were truly helpless, and you learned to endure until the abuse passed. That survival strategy made sense then. But now as an adult who can get away from danger, this isn't keeping you safe; it's keeping you stuck. The trouble is, you don't feel like an adult. When you can recognize the cycle of abuse you are in (or keep getting into), you can learn to break it. Safe people can show you how to grow into a powerful adult who sets boundaries and holds them.

Learn to Ground Yourself to Stay Present Because you were abused and coerced into things, you may have learned to dissociate. But now that keeps you stuck in compliance and unable to see you have adult rights that could be used to get you (and any children) to safety.

When you dissociate, not only does this expose you to abuse, it can further abuse of your children by removing the protective adult—you—from the situation. You can be the adult now that you wanted to go to for help as a child. Learn some mindfulness techniques to keep you grounded to the present moment, so you don't mentally check out when danger is approaching. As you learn to keep your mind connected to your body, you can better see the abuse happening or about to happen, and do something about it.

Know the Cycle of Abuse In cases of domestic violence or sexual abuse, the pattern is often more visible because physical harm is involved. But when the abuse is emotional, verbal, or psychological, it can be much harder to identify—and easier to minimize. For example, someone may not view a chronically angry partner as abusive, yet the underlying destructive cycle is often the same:

Stage 1. The Tension-Building You begin to feel like you're walking on eggshells trying to avoid triggering your partner's anger—doing whatever it takes to appease them and keep the peace. Sometimes, you may even provoke the conflict just to control when and how the explosion happens—anything to lessen the impact.

Stage 2. The Incident This is when the abuse happens. It may be physical, sexual, verbal, psychological, or emotional—ranging from threats, accusations, name-calling, shaming, to physical harm or coercion. Regardless of the form it takes, abuse is always about power and control.

Stage 3. The Reconciliation After the incident, the abuser may apologize, beg for forgiveness, make promises to change, give gifts, show affection or express their love in dramatic ways. They may seem remorseful, even loving. You might feel temporarily relieved or even empowered for having "gotten through it." In this stage the power dynamic often temporarily flips, and the Victim can feel in control. But this stage is strategic—designed to keep you emotionally hooked and hesitant to leave or seek help.

Stage 4. The Calm ("Honeymoon" Stage) Things return to normal or even seem better than before. The abuser may act kind, affectionate, or supportive—almost like nothing happened. This false peace can bring hope. But unfortunately, this phase is temporary. The tension begins to build again, and the cycle starts over.

Many victims feel trapped: bound by spiritual beliefs that discourage leaving marriages, fear of losing their children or their abuser having some custody of their children without them being present, financial dependence, or shame. Abusers often reinforce this trap by convincing their partners that they are the problem, and that they caused the abuse. This keeps victims trying to figure out how to improve and keep from making the abuser mad again, which of course isn't possible. You are never responsible for someone else's abusive behavior. Recognizing the cycle is the first step toward breaking free from it.

Speak Up and Get to Safety As children, Victims learned to silently endure suffering because they had no other choice. Over time, this became their "normal," which is why so many stay in unbearable situations without realizing they deserve better. But abuse is never acceptable. It is always wrong and should never be tolerated.

You deserve safety, healing, and support. A trusted therapist can help you understand what a healthy relationship looks like and guide you in finding the courage to get yourself, and any children, to safety.

Many communities offer help through domestic violence shelters and resource centers. These often provide free support groups, empowerment programs, and safe housing. In these spaces you'll meet others with similar stories, and begin to realize you're not alone. Shelter locations are typically kept confidential to ensure your safety and prevent a controlling partner from finding you.

Some family law firms offer free (pro bono) legal aid for domestic violence victims, while some police departments facilitate free safety classes that teach basic self-defense skills. By just learning some of these basic skills, it can give you confidence to *take action*. Once you are empowered, you can become a survivor and never have to be a victim again.

Establish Boundaries Victims often aren't respected because they were never taught how to push back, maintain firm limits, or hold others accountable for their bad behavior. When your cries for help went unanswered, you learned you couldn't stop the harm being done to you. You were robbed of your voice, and your boundaries were not respected so you stopped believing you can have any.

Learning to say "No" and "Stop" *with conviction* is necessary to protect yourself and any children. You will need to practice this to learn how to assert yourself and hold your ground. Learning to assert yourself is essential for protecting both you and your children. This takes practice. Working with a trusted therapist or support group in role-playing scenarios can help you build this skill in a safe space. These exercises allow your nervous system to practice what it feels like to stand your ground, turning fear into justice-fueled strength. This helps rewire your brain—shifting from a "fawn" (freeze or appease) reaction to a healthy "fight" response when necessary. Boundaries are not just helpful; they are essential for healthy relationships. As you learn to set and enforce yours, you'll begin to feel stronger, more confident, and more in control. You'll discover that standing up for yourself and protecting your children is not only possible—it's your right.

Practice Makes Progress

No matter your attachment style, when you accept that growth, by its nature, is uncomfortable, even painful sometimes, you can know you are already progressing. And your resistance will fade the more you practice.

Consider ranking your growth areas from most difficult to least difficult. This ranking will help you prioritize and focus on your most challenging areas. Next take your top five areas and put them on the "dashboard" of your life—set alerts on your phone, sticky notes on your bathroom mirror, reminders on your laptop or other visible places—to stay mindful of them throughout the day. This prompting will help you stay aware to identify the triggers as they creep up on you and remind you to practice the secure replacement behaviors. Remember, good relationships happen on purpose, not by accident. And you can only consciously change something you are consciously aware of. Once you notice it, you can change it! We're going to look at how each attachment style can form resistance to growth next.

> **REFLECT**
>
> 1. What are your top areas of growth?
>
> 2. Are you willing to ask those closest to you: *"Which one of these growth goals would make the biggest difference to our relationship?"*

Chapter Eleven

Resistance

You've likely heard the term "resistance training," which is used in exercise to increase muscle strength by purposely pushing against an equal opposing force to increase endurance. It's a similar thing when we begin exercising our vulnerability muscles for the first time. The more you counter-resist against your self-protective reactive strategies by working your growth goals, you gradually increase your ability to employ more secure strategies, and momentum will build.

But like working out at the gym, it's always easier not to do it than to show up and put in the hard work. And it's easy to find excuses to justify doing so. Doing nothing, however, keeps you weak and in broken relationships because our reactive neural pathways are our current default and require no thought or effort. Making others adjust to us is easier and less painful than growing, and your insecure attachment style has a strong magnetic pull that will want to resist your efforts. So, *your current reactive strategies will resist your growth*, until you apply counter-resistance. If you choose not to, you'll be stuck before you even begin.

> So, *your current reactive strategies will resist your growth*, until you apply counter-resistance.

Being overwhelmed by powerful emotions such as fear, resentment, and shame makes even the toughest among us believe we aren't capable. It might seem unfair that we have to work so hard to grow when it was others who hurt us.

But in your goal of earning secure attachment, feeling resistant is an indicator you're pushing against a deep protective strategy your mind believes is still the only way to keep you safe. And like in resistance training, pressing in is how you'll grow. Those negative emotions are not the enemy. *Emotions are indicators, not dictators.* They often tell us about how we've been wounded, and learning to listen and respond to them is how we grow. When we can come to manage our emotions, rather than suppress them or let them spill out into dictating our actions, we find freedom. Trading old insecure, reactive self-protective strategies for more adaptive responses modifies your neural pathways with experiences that make you feel self-controlled and more secure.

> Feeling resistant is an indicator you're pushing against a deep protective strategy your mind believes is still the only way to keep you safe.

Each insecure attachment type has its specific resistance against growing toward secure attachment. Every long-distance runner at some point has "hit the wall" during a race, when their body runs out of energy and they think they can't go any further. Their body actually can, it's simply switching energy sources to run off stored fats and proteins because it's exhausted the current energy source it was using. You need to know the ways this can happen for your insecure attachment style so you can be ready to face your "walls." Not understanding this may leave you disconnected and unfulfilled, reasoning these growth strategies don't work, or are too hard. However, equipped with the knowledge in this chapter, you'll be prepared for this challenge, and know you can get a joy surge back as you push through your resistance toward your future securely attached self waiting at the finish line.

> Emotions are indicators, not dictators.

Avoider Resistance

Darren grew up with one abusive parent and one dismissive parent. His father often took out his frustration on him when he was very young. When his mother filed for divorce, Darren was four years old, and the abuse came to light. Darren's father left the country before the authorities could get involved, and Darren never saw him again.

Darren didn't receive any counseling for the abuse, as it wasn't as readily available back then. His mother tried her best raising two boys but had no family support of her own. A child of parents who sent her to the US at fourteen for a better life, she had grown up with her grandmother, who was no longer alive. Growing up, Darren's mother was often absent, working two jobs. Even so, they struggled with financial hardship, living in a low-income farming community. Darren and his brother both contributed with chores and worked part-time jobs while they were in high school. With no other family support available, Darren was left largely to raise himself and his brother alone.

When his mother was around, Darren didn't receive much physical comfort or tender words from her. This wasn't intentional on her part; she just did not know how to give what she hadn't received herself. Darren knew his mother loved him though. And because she grew up in extreme poverty and with no family, Darren and his brother also knew they were fortunate even in the little they had. Darren learned being strong and staying positive helped his mother. And while it gave him a good attitude toward life, he'd become an Avoider who was highly performance-based.

> Each attachment type has specific resistance against growth.

Darren didn't think he needed much help, but his wife insisted they come for couples therapy, seeking a deeper emotional connection with him. When he came in, he claimed he'd already processed on his own the childhood abuse that he disclosed on the intake paperwork. It didn't impact him, so we didn't need to "go there," he said. He had few memories of it, being so young, and he didn't want to remember anyway. He also didn't understand why talking about his childhood or identifying if he was sad or feeling overwhelmed mattered. He appreciated the hardships he'd endured because he perceived these had made him strong and these characteristics were now helping him in his career. He didn't see how talking about that would help him connect more with his wife. He reasoned, men are supposed to be strong providers, and that's what he was doing. He was faithful, hard-working, and loved his wife, so what can't she connect with in that?

For many understandable reasons, Darren was *resistant*.

Many Avoiders use "reaction formation," a defense mechanism using exaggerated opposite reactions when they feel uncomfortable, such as laughing or smiling when talking about something painful. It's often subconscious. Darren refused to acknowledge his abuse and how his mother's dismissal and lack of comfort negatively impacted him. When I asked how he felt, he smiled and acted nonplussed, thinking I was asking him to manufacture negative emotions.

The irony with Avoiders is, you can often explain all the logical neuroscience of how humans are designed to be emotional beings, but because they have no personal reference of what it feels like to be "emotional," they don't truly comprehend it. You must be open to feeling to understand emotions, and when Avoiders resist doing so, they block that understanding.

The following are often where Avoiders get stuck:

- Being avoidant, hyper-independent, and self-reliant continues to serve a purpose in adulthood to succeed at work or dull pain, so Avoiders aren't motivated to change their reactive strategies because they like this about themselves.
- Avoiders struggle to notice secondary emotions under anger, frustration, and irritation. They can be blind to more vulnerable emotions—shame, sadness, fear, and feeling

overwhelmed—and so think they don't really experience these.
- Avoiders can believe those who experience vulnerable emotions are less resilient to life's challenges. These Avoiders reason that if secure attachment means feeling vulnerable emotions, this would weaken rather than strengthen them, and so don't understand why that would be good.
- Their identity is often rooted in their accomplishments, and dulling emotions helps Avoiders "get over" things to be more productive. They may believe they'll be wasting time learning to experience deeper emotions and it will slow them down.
- Avoiders reflexively laugh off their feelings or end interactions with sarcasm, quickly dismissing before they can even notice emotions. This blocks them from developing emotional self-awareness.
- Avoiders typically see negative emotions as the source of relationship problems and what makes people not in control. They label others who outwardly display strong feelings as being "too emotional"—even if someone is simply responding vulnerably. When they hold this view they can reason, "If I feel more emotions, my relationships will just have more problems." For them, gaining emotional awareness is not a benefit if having emotions are not beneficial.
- Having their lack of emotional competency exposed in therapy makes Avoiders feel inadequate. When their efforts are criticized by a spouse they often deny vulnerable feelings, clam up, or hide behind anger.
- Some Avoiders can embrace their insecure attachment style as "the way they are" to excuse them from growing. They believe their distancing and lack of emotions and emotional awareness are simply part of their personality or nature that others need to accept.

When Avoiders embrace their insecurities and resist growth, they set a double standard of expecting others to change "to not be reactive" while they don't have to, because they don't see their avoidance as being reactive. But when Avoiders can recognize their resistant excuses, and practice pushing against them, they build capacity to feel. And because feelings allow you to have the full human experience, they will start to realize there's a whole side of life they've been missing out on.

Pleaser Resistance

In the eight months since Lisa and her husband had started therapy with me, they'd made little progress. She was still bailing her son out of trouble as she had since he was a child. Now at thirty-two, and struggling with addiction, he was enjoying their help paying his rent and bills since he couldn't seem to hold down a job. Shielded from consequences, he had no motivation to change, and Lisa didn't see how her actions were anything less than what any "loving mother" would do for her struggling son.

Lisa had grown up with fearful parents, though her mother didn't see herself as so. As a high school teacher her mother had once written a book report for Lisa when she had procrastinated over it because she felt overwhelmed by the assignment. Her main focus was Lisa getting into a good college, and she couldn't tolerate failing grades. This model was reinforced by Lisa's father who worked in insurance. He was a cautious man, focused on risk mitigation at work and in family life. He gave Lisa all she needed so she did not to have to work until she was done with college. Lack of facing challenges and modeling of codependency caused Lisa to develop a Pleaser attachment style, and now she was repeating the lessons for her adult son. Lisa's husband was exasperated by her codependency with their son. He attempted natural consequences, to withhold help so their son would have to answer to his financial commitments, but Lisa would frequently go behind his back and cancel out his efforts.

Lisa couldn't bear to watch her son struggle or face the consequences for his inaction, even though she knew they were necessary for him to develop resiliency. His "suffering" drove her anxiety, which was overwhelming for her. And while she did not admit it, rescuing him was her easiest way to reduce her anxiety, instead of the more challenging task of learning to tolerate and manage it.

Pleasers often see stress as bad—for themselves and others. However, some stress is actually necessary for our growth. Normative stress occurs from ordinary life experiences we all have that are not dangerous or threatening—such as feeling nervous about what to expect on the first day of school, the anxiety of your parent letting go when learning how to swim or ride a bike, or relational challenges with peers and teachers at school. Managing, rather than avoiding, such stress helps us learn unpleasant experiences are not unsolvable. Confidence is polar to anxiety, and true confidence is only gained through experience of overcoming trials.

The following are often where Pleasers get stuck:

- Pleasers are conditioned to be fearful. Since fear is one of our strongest primal drivers, Pleasers resist doing the practical work of "exposure" that is needed to overcome fears and build the new neural pathways that only develop from experience.
- The Pleaser's sense of who they are is typically grounded in a relationship with their parent, partner, or children. Pleasers can fear they may lose their identity if they stop being codependent, and this keeps them from establishing a strong individual identity that can separate their feelings from the feelings of others.
- Pleasers are often unable to resist and hold boundaries when others are distressed, angry, or disappointed in them, which keeps them enmeshed and pleasing, reinforcing the very pattern they need to break.

- Pleasers tend to avoid conversations to confront, which are needed to create the tension for growth to occur. They don't realize deeper trust and intimacy will develop through loving confrontation, so they continue the path of least resistance to their detriment.
- Because they caretake, take on others' pain, and are too easily influenced by others' emotions, Pleasers can have a hard time identifying or holding onto an independent perspective, making it hard for others who want to help the Pleaser know what the Pleaser really wants.

When Pleasers are too fearful to grow, they inadvertently place all the responsibility on others, which continues the negative cycle they desperately want to end. When they can expose themselves to the situations they fear and see these are not deadly, they can slowly build tolerance muscles and gain confidence to stand strong, even when others show displeasure toward them.

Vacillator Resistance

Olivia and James were the most typical attachment combination I see in couples therapy. Olivia had a Vacillator attachment style and James an Avoider style. They presented the usual dynamic, with Olivia wanting more connection from James and protesting by getting angry, sulking, or distancing to try and get him to come after her. James saw her as overreacting and dramatic. Why did she have to be so "emotional," and why couldn't she just be logical like him? He'd distance more when Olivia would protest, waiting for her to "stop being so childish," which left her feeling more alone and angry—and so the cycle repeated.

One session, they arrived in a conflict that had gone unresolved for days. Olivia's anxiety and anger had been building while she was giving him the silent treatment, waiting for our session when she'd finally have his attention to "tell him how he had hurt her." James looked uncomfortable knowing he was trapped and couldn't avoid the discussion any longer. I attempted to guide them through a conversation using the Comfort Circle, with Olivia as the speaker to start. This quickly went sideways. Her anger was thick, and she was resistant to dig underneath it for the more vulnerable emotions that James could have practiced empathizing with. When I tried to help her say something James could connect with, she blurted, *"Anyone would feel this way! The words you want me to use don't sound like me. I can't be fake! I'm sorry, I prefer to be real."*

To her, learning to rein in her reactive anger and use more secure phrases felt restrictive and phony. Vacillators want connection they can feel, and they want it to be genuine. If words or actions from others don't come willingly and quickly, or don't seem empathetic enough, they tend to reject the entire effort.

The following are often where Vacillators get stuck:

- They focus primarily on how they've been hurt—often feeling their pain is greater or more deserving—so expect their feelings to be given greater importance when trying to resolve a conflict. Their zeal to be understood exceeds their willingness to understand, which leaves others feeling stuck in the unfairness that the Vacillator expects more than they, themselves, are willing to give.
- Because Vacillators don't like to wait, they typically want to share their feelings and perspectives first and struggle to hear others out if they have not yet had their turn or been agreed with. This imbalance often prevents conflict resolution.
- Vacillators can have a hard time respecting another's right to hold opposing views, and can feel that validating and empathizing with others is giving in, even though the Vacillator

requires this from others. Others then don't feel heard or understood.
- Vacillators can become frustrated if others aren't growing quickly enough for them, which keeps the focus off their own growth. They may demand others change before they're willing to, which creates a contract mindset that makes it okay for them to react when they perceive the other as not doing their part.
- Disappointment over efforts that are not done smoothly because the other person is still learning skills can make the Vacillator interpret efforts as disingenuous or "robotic," and so they sabotage the connection. This leaves the other person disheartened and hesitant to try again.
- Because Vacillators tend toward emotional reasoning, feelings determine truth for them. They can be very stubborn if they have decided they are the most injured party in a circumstance or once they have made up their mind to leave a relationship. All-or-nothing thinking causes them to believe they can't be happy with that person again because the hurt from the offenses are insurmountable. These Vacillators struggle to see how their future healed self might be able to forgive and love again from a more secure lens, or acknowledge that their anger and protests have caused hurts that are equally valid to the other person who also needs to forgive much.

Others around Vacillators may grow tired over double standards, always having to listen to the Vacillator first, not really being heard out, being expected to agree with them, or having their efforts rejected. If others hold boundaries or show displeasure, the Vacillator often digs in harder, which ultimately exacerbates the negative cycle. Yet once Vacillators can become aware of the origins of their wounds and notice their reactive patterns, they can make remarkable growth. And when they seek relational balance, they can find the emotionally healthy connection they so desperately desire.

Controller Resistance

Lucas and Charlotte were stuck in an abusive relationship dynamic. Charlotte was a Controller and Lucas was a Victim. Both had grown up in abusive environments and had developed Disorganized attachments. Charlotte's mother didn't know who Charlotte's father was. She was an addict and often intoxicated, exposing Charlotte to physical and sexual abuse by many of her boyfriends she brought home. Eventually, the addiction led to homelessness, and Charlotte, her mother, and her siblings lived in a tent under a freeway, eating ketchup packets from fast food restaurants as their meals.

One day Charlotte and her siblings were left for several hours in a fast-food play place and Child Protective Services was called. She was separated from her younger siblings in foster care, and being over nine, as with many children that age in the foster system, she was never adopted. The pain of being separated and feeling unwanted, along with her abuse, left Charlotte replaying her trauma frequently. There were some placements where she would have liked to stay, but her outbursts of rage made her unsafe around other children, and eventually foster parents couldn't cope. Enduring fourteen placements by the time she turned eighteen, Charlotte aged out of foster care as a very angry young adult with no modeled strategies of how to self-soothe or talk herself through pain or disappointment.

Lucas, who grew up in fear of his mother's rages if he wasn't quiet enough for her, couldn't understand as a child why his mother beat him for minor infractions. A personality disorder made her impossible to please, and it seemed like neither he nor anyone could do anything to fill the empty hole she had inside. His father, a Pleaser, couldn't stand up to her, and as an only child, Lucas was often left alone with her when his father went to work. He felt frequently helpless against his mother's raging and unrealistic expectations of him.

Given their significant childhood traumas, therapy was challenging from the start. Since they were also getting individual help, I had agreed to see them together under the special condition of a safety agreement where they committed to my zero-tolerance for abuse to do conjoint therapy as well as giving me permission to collaborate with their individual therapists. When they came to me they had described that when Charlotte would get into a rage, she would throw things and yell at Lucas, stop him from leaving the room, and ridicule him for "not being a man." Conditioned to endure such extreme rage, Lucas felt helpless, arguing back at times, but always ending up giving in. They had managed to abide by these rules for the first few weeks; however, one day Charlotte went into a rant and caught Lucas subtly trying to record her on his phone. She flew into a rage. During the scuffle to get the phone, she scratched his face badly. Neighbors had already called the police, and when they saw Lucas's face, Charlotte went to jail for the night.

This was Lucas's chance to create a boundary with a forced separation. If he filed for a restraining order, the judge would grant it. Charlotte would be ordered to an anger management class—as is typical in these situations for a first-time offender—and need to demonstrate progress to avoid a more serious charge. Faced with the consequences, Charlotte apologized profusely and promised never to do it again. Lucas declined to press charges and she was released.

The following are typically what stop Controllers from growing:

- Controllers are used to giving the orders and don't like others giving them advice, so they resist seeking help. They typically only attend therapy if it's court ordered, they're awaiting legal charges and are hoping for a lighter sentence, when people in their social communities (such as a church) discover their abuse, or if the victim is about to leave them.

- People who experience abuse or other trauma in childhood have an increased risk of developing personality disorders and intermittent explosive disorder.* Controllers may need medication, a sponsor, or a support group to help them calm their intensity and slow down their reactivity to do the practice work. Many Controllers see these options as weakness and are unlikely to seek this help.
- Addictions are often the way Controllers and Victims medicate their emotional pain. Addictions demand one's allegiance, and dependence and numbing prevent the person from working on their attachment injury. Recovery groups are usually needed to help break this, though an addict often has to hit rock bottom before they are willing to attend. Relapse is also often part of the recovery process, and many recovery programs only focus on sobriety, and not on the source of the emotional pain driving the addiction. So, recovery groups alone are often not enough.
- Controllers may refuse to acknowledge their abuse of others if it's not as bad as what they experienced or if it's not sexual or physical in nature.

Sadly, many Controllers don't get the help they need, because they are the least likely to seek it. People are also less likely to help Controllers than they are Victims. However, when Controllers can build trust with people who care and are willing to come alongside and support them, they can grieve and finally heal from their painful past.

---

* Erin C. Berenz et al., "Childhood Trauma and Personality Disorder Criterion Counts: A Co-Twin Control Analysis," *Journal of Abnormal Psychology* 122, no. 4 (2013): 1070–1076, https://doi.org/10.1037/a0034238; Annemarie F. Reardon et al., "Intermittent Explosive Disorder: Associations with PTSD and Other Axis I Disorders in a US Military Veteran Sample," *Journal of Anxiety Disorders* 28, no. 5 (2014): 488–494, https://doi.org/10.1016/j.janxdis.2014.05.001.

Victim Resistance

The following are typically what prevent Victims from growing:

- Earning secure attachment is impossible when in an abusive relationship. But Victims often go back to their abuser repeatedly and are unwilling to break the cycle, even when offered a way out. Most Victims need a strong relationship with a therapist to build trust they'll have support if they do leave, and some need years of work in therapy before they're strong enough to do so. Unfortunately, many therapists give up on Victims before they get to this point due to a perceived lack of progress.
- When Victims are fearful of serious harm if they leave, it can be nearly impossible to convince them to do so, especially if children may be forced into shared custody.
- Many Victims involuntarily deal with their trauma through dissociation, making them less likely to be able to process it. Since processing their trauma is the only way to earn secure attachment, many need medication and/or a trauma-based therapy to get them out of a freeze reaction before they can learn to hold healthy boundaries. Sadly, not all get this help.

Growing up with a dangerous caregiver, Victims often have few, or no, healthy loving experiences to build upon for a template of healthy attachment. When people who are willing to support the Victim can understand the cycle of abuse and be patient with them, Victims can learn what supportive and loving relationships should look like and be empowered to break the cycle. Rewiring entrenched neural pathways is an intentional process though, which we will look at in the next chapter.

REFLECT

1. Which ways do you see yourself justifying insecurities that stifle your growth?

2. Is it easier to recognize areas needing growth in others than to admit ways you remain stuck?

3. What resistance can you commit to overcoming, even when others don't do their part?

4. Who do you trust to hold you accountable to address your resistance so you can "show up to practice"?

Chapter Twelve

Rewiring Neural Pathways

With billions of neurons in a human brain, whenever we have an experience, neurons associated with elements of that experience fire and wire together to form a pathway. We then assign meaning to that experience, which predicts our future behavior. Imagine driving in an unfamiliar place and you approach and then stop at a red traffic light. You've never seen this traffic light before or been down this road, but because of prior experiences, you expect it will soon turn green, like every other traffic light you've encountered before. After a while waiting, you think, *Surely this is going to turn green any second now.* You're tempted to go through it because you have an appointment and no one else is around. But you wait, just in case something bad were to happen. In this instance, your past is predicting your current behavior.

Like roadways in the brain, neural pathways have the same scenery, weather, road conditions, and traffic patterns every time they're travelled. The road is marked with "Situation—Emotion—Bodily Feeling—Need—Action—Belief" and eventually, each neural pathway arrives at a particular location. These six elements get wired together from experiences of events, people, places, and most everything we encounter in life. Our initial experiences of a situation involve emotions and bodily feelings, perceived corresponding needs, and what actions helped us either get those needs met or deal with them being unmet.

Depending on how significant or frequent this experience is, a self-protective reaction may form along with a self-belief about how likely it is the need will be met in the future with that person or situation. As the pathway gets fused together, it may only take a reencounter of one of these six things to trigger the domino effect of the whole neural pathway refiring. Our adaptive brains make shortcuts using associations to help us learn, and repeated or significant experiences further cement these pathways.

> Our adaptive brains make shortcuts using associations to help us learn.

For repeated experiences, picture a roadway-widening project. The more we travel that road, the more lanes and entrance ramps we add to that roadway, making it easier to join and travel down. Eventually the thing we keep doing becomes muscle memory and we do it subconsciously—just like the old saying about riding a bike! This can be both beneficial and detrimental. I can drive home using subconscious processes while simultaneously consciously focusing my thoughts on something more important. On the flip side, subconscious processes make it incredibly hard to break negative habits, like biting your nails.

When it comes to significant experiences, especially negative ones, it can take only one to overpower many other benign experiences. Let's say while going through an intersection during your right of way you get hit by another car that runs a light. Even though you've had thousands of experiences of nothing bad happening when you obeyed the rules of road this way, this *one* experience could impact how hesitant you are next time at that intersection, or any intersection, or anytime you drive at all. While retravelling neural pathways of positive experiences helps lift our spirits, excites us, or injects confidence, others built by negative experiences can cause over-reactivity, regardless of the true threat in a circumstance (like Oliver with his girlfriend's small dog in Chapter 3).

What's Your Anchor?

Intentionally changing certain elements in a neural pathway is a way we can construct diversions in these existing roadways, which will in turn create a new neural pathway. Applying bitter nail polish can stop the subconscious activity of nail-biting by retraining your brain that fingers taste unpleasant. However, emotions are not as easily changed because emotions create needs. We can change these pathways more effectively by influencing the other elements—bodily feelings, behaviors, thoughts, and beliefs.

One way to change bodily feelings when panicking is breathing into a paper bag. Shallow breaths prepare us for "fight or flight" activity, yet this can also unbalance concentrations of oxygen and carbon dioxide in the blood, making you feel lightheaded or faint. Breathing into a paper bag causes you to rebreathe carbon dioxide, stabilizing blood concentration levels. It also regulates the filling of your lungs to slow your heart pumping adrenaline throughout your body. Calming your body in this way can reduce your emotion of panic.

We can also change a situation by having scripts to say (like I gave you in the attachment chapters) or by practicing new behaviors (such as growth goals) when certain stimuli happen. This is why role-play is such a great way to learn holding boundaries, because it gives you a similar experience in a safe place and with a safe person, thereby changing the neural pathway. Even just learning to pause before reacting can help us notice our thoughts so we can examine them.

> We can also change a situation by having scripts to say or by practicing new behaviors.

But how do we change our beliefs? I can't, for example, choose not to believe in gravity, because all my experiences show it to be true. In the same way, it's hard to change my values, even when convenient (like at tax time). Beliefs are like anchors fixing us to a spot. They tie us to our emotions and subsequent needs, which then produces our behaviors. And like any anchor, beliefs *can either sink us or save us*. Insecure beliefs drag us down into the depths of insecurity with them. Some insecure beliefs that can sink us are *"Making mistakes means I'm defective,"* or *"It's shameful to ask for help to meet my needs,"* or *"When things go wrong it must mean I am to blame."* In stark contrast, secure beliefs can save us by keeping us securely grounded, even during the storms of life. These beliefs sound like *"I am lovable and valuable despite my mistakes,"* or *"Everyone deserves to be respected, including me."*

> Secure beliefs can save us by keeping us securely grounded, even during the storms of life.

When our bodies develop harmful growths, like cancer, we need to either surgically remove them or shrink them through treatment until they're no longer a threat. We can take the same approach with insecure beliefs. By consciously noticing them and intentionally challenging them, we can begin to shrink their influence to systematically eliminate them over time. This process helps create new, healthier experiences for the brain. It's even more effective in this process when others come alongside us with love, comfort, and support, because their presence adds a positive emotional element to help divert the neural pathway.

Beliefs are so hard to change because they're deeply ingrained, and often in the subconscious. When you drive you don't usually think about whether your brakes are going to work. You believe they will until you have an experience that shows you otherwise. This leads you to have an unconscious self-belief of "I am safe." Conversely, any experience that taught you that you weren't safe leads you to have an insecure belief, even when it's not rational. To change insecure beliefs, we must become conscious of them so we can cut off these anchors and replace them with more helpful, secure ones. That requires deciding what secure belief to grab hold of instead, so we can confidently let the insecure one go.

It takes great intention to hack away at these anchors, and you'll need to persuade yourself to make the effort if you want to form secure beliefs. As you do this, it's important to recognize that your emotions and bodily feelings may take more time to change than your reasoning. But they will follow as you create new experiences with safe people and in safe environments to cement your new beliefs. Consider some of these examples of secure beliefs replacing insecure ones:

Insecure belief: "Crying means I am attention-seeking."
Secure belief: "It's okay to cry. Crying is how we're designed to get our pain out."

Insecure belief: "I shouldn't feel hurt about this."
Secure belief: "My pain is real, and I am allowed to feel it."

Insecure belief: "I am shameful. Things are my fault, and I deserve bad things to happen to me."
Secure belief: "Actions are good or bad, not people. Mistakes are allowed and how people learn and grow. Making mistakes does not mean I'm undeserving of love."

Insecure belief: "I should be nice and not do things that upset others, even if they hurt me."
Secure belief: "I should be loving, and love sets appropriate limits on destructive behavior."

Insecure belief: "When others are upset, I'm responsible to fix the problem so they can feel better."
Secure belief: "When others are upset, my job is to comfort if I can and it's their responsibility to manage their emotions and problem-solve."

Insecure belief: "Conflict is upsetting and bad, so we should always avoid it."

Secure belief: "Conflict is normal and it can be an opportunity to grow closer through repair and understanding of each other's views."

Insecure belief: "Negative emotions are bad since they make people irrational, and this means you are weak."
Secure belief: "Emotions indicate needs that can be met and comforted. It's healthy to be balanced, with both logic and emotions."

Insecure belief: "When people don't pay attention to my needs, I have to yell and act out to get them to see me and respond."
Secure belief: "When others don't listen or respond to my needs, I will be okay. I can make clear requests or hold healthy boundaries in ways that invite connection."

Insecure belief: "Others hurt me too much for me to stay connected."
Secure belief: "When I'm hurt, I can self-soothe to recover, and reconnection is possible in repair, even if it feels uncomfortable."

Insecure belief: "When others don't see things my way, they must think I'm bad or dumb."
Secure belief: "Differences of opinions are normal and not rejections of me."

Insecure belief: "When others don't understand, I can't connect with them."
Secure belief: "Secure connection accepts and respects seeing things differently."

Reframing

Learning to be aware of what we're thinking, and of the patterns behind it, is called metacognition. In his book *Breath by Breath*,[*] author Larry Rosenberg contrasts lions' and dogs' minds when it comes to perceived distractions, which helps illustrate what it means to see beyond our thoughts and emotions. He says, if you wave a bone in front of a dog, the dog fixates on the bone. And if you toss it to the side, the dog chases it down. But a lion is not so distracted. The reason the lion does not fixate on the bone or chase after it is because the lion is more interested in you!

When we get stuck concentrating on our unhelpful thoughts and insecure beliefs, we are fixated on our insecurity. Noticing the "bone" in front of us is acknowledging reality, but chasing the bone is woeful.

You can learn to do the following instead when you're triggered:

- Notice your thoughts and feelings
- Hold back your urge to react
- Think "Where have I felt this before?"
- Identify associations between the present situation and your original wounding event
- Acknowledge this is an old neural pathway
- Focus on the creation and strengthening of the new neural pathway

In therapy, we call changing the way you think about something *reframing*. The situation and outcome remain the same, but learning to reframe your thinking by changing your internal dialogue from negative to positive can help you to develop a better self-belief and think with more balance.

---

[*] Larry Rosenberg with David Guy, *Breath by Breath: The Liberating Practice of Insight Meditation* (Shambhala, 2015).

> Changing your internal dialogue from negative to positive can help you to develop a better self-belief.

Melissa, a Pleaser, had a negative belief of "It's always my fault," formed by repeated messages from her parents blaming and shaming her during her childhood. Today she owns a moderately sized successful company, and we had been working on her building confidence to give constructive feedback to her employees, as a boss needs to at times. During one session, she came in distressed after she had to address a costly mistake made by a friend who she'd hired. This friend was upset and told her, "Your words really hurt me," which triggered Melissa's negative self-belief. I helped Melissa reframe the interaction: It wasn't what she said that hurt her friend, but what her friend heard.

Melissa had been brave enough to tell the truth, and that had stung her friend. Not because Melissa's words were reckless, but likely because they hit a nerve of her friend's own historical emotional wound with a negative self-belief. The feedback was more like antiseptic in an open wound. You can blame the doctor for applying the treatment because it hurts, or you can see that it only hurts because you have an injury. Melissa's friend took what Melissa said as harm because of her own unresolved insecurities, not because what Melissa said was mean or inappropriate. As Melissa reframed this event, it did not change what happened or the outcome, but it helped her see she didn't do anything wrong and wasn't to blame for her friend's feelings.

Sometimes, the hardest thing to change about ourselves is the way we see things. To earn secure attachment, you will need to learn to capture and reexamine your thoughts to reframe your perceptions.

If Changing the Belief Seems Impossible

Chloe came to therapy because she had started a new job three months prior and was noticing strong reactions to her new boss. Anytime he'd raise his voice even slightly, Chloe would go into a flight and freeze reaction inside—feeling panicky and needing to leave the room, but frozen like she couldn't escape. Being in a competitive and demanding field, most of her coworkers appeared unmoved by their boss's antics, knowing it was part of the territory that came with the job, and that there were pressures from his superiors he had to manage. As a supervisor, Chloe had to review the sales report with him every Friday afternoon. And if it wasn't favorable, he made his annoyance clear.

Since Chloe's childhood had been traumatic, I suspected it was a trigger. Her parents divorced when she was three, sharing custody. Her father was avoidant, focusing his attention on his new wife, while Chloe's mother had a personality disorder and her behavior was unpredictable. She was sometimes kind and other times raged, drinking until she passed out.

These binges terrified Chloe, and she'd hide in the bathroom cabinet until her mother stopped screaming. When Chloe was ten, Child Protective Services took her away, but the emotional damage was significant. Her sympathetic nervous system rang a loud internal alarm bell anytime she heard a raised voice. Her insecure anchor belief was *"I'm helpless and too weak to change my situation."*

As I helped Chloe make the link to feeling stuck in a room with her boss and her experiences with her mother, she began to see how her insecure attachment style formed, but we found it wasn't enough to try changing her negative messages into positive ones that would calm her body. So, I used a trauma-based approach called Eye Movement Desensitization and Reprocessing (EMDR) therapy, which helps people identify and reprocess emotional experiences when powerful memories are causing significant distress. Since all reactions are "re-actions"—a repeat of actions that were once the most adaptive strategy we could find—processing a memory to reduce the intensity of our current reaction requires identifying and reprocessing from the original stimulus. These are called "touchstone memories," and they helped us get to what was setting off Chloe's internal alarm bell.

During the desensitization process, Chloe was able to revisit and re-experience the original memory, knowing she was safe in the therapy room. We worked on calming her body and installing a more secure anchor belief: *"I'm an adult now, and in control of my environment. I am stronger and have the power to change my situation."* I guided her through imagining herself going back into her childhood home as her adult self and rescuing that little girl who was small and powerless when her mom raged. Adult Chloe went to the cabinet under the bathroom sink and picked up her younger self, who clung to her. She then walked down the stairs and out the door to safety. In doing this, Chloe formed a new association to this memory of being empowered, strong, and capable of changing her environment.

As touchstone memories are processed, the threat-detection amygdala works with the hippocampus to consolidate the memory. These are eventually transferred to the neocortex for long-term storage to become narrative memories of *past* events. This transfer process is thought to occur particularly during rapid eye movement (REM) sleep cycles, and EMDR bilateral stimulation techniques are thought to mimic this natural processing. By doing the mental role-play during EMDR, we retrained Chloe's amygdala to assign positive emotional tags to this memory so that her prefrontal cortex would handle her response actions from now on. While future events might feel similar, the emotional significance to the touchstone memory had now been changed, and Chloe could now perceive she is not the same small, helpless child she once was.

After that, Chloe was calmer around her boss. We also practiced some verbal scripts she could use to redirect him to communicating his frustrations more calmly. The first time she tried it, he didn't calm down, so Chloe left and said she'd return when he could. He was shocked, and likely fearing an HR complaint, he apologized. Though his irritability continued in staff meetings, the individual meetings with Chloe were different from then on. The new memory and belief from EMDR helped her to feel empowered to create a new narrative and anchor belief about herself to change her environment.

I've walked many clients through reprocessing distressing experiences with EMDR, and I highly recommend finding a qualified therapist if you've been working on the same struggles for a while with limited success in reducing your reactivity.

Repairing significant relational wounds is never easy work. Yet repair is the only way to truly progress a relationship that has been damaged, and it's another vital way to change memories and overcome negative beliefs. As we'll see next, nothing short of a full engagement in the process of relational repair and forgiveness can lead to deep recovery of security in you and your relationships.

REFLECT

1. Have you developed a "lion" mind—one that can stay grounded by noticing and naming emotions and thought patterns? Or do you find yourself with more like a "dog" mind, easily pulled along and distracted by whatever your emotions and thoughts are doing in the moment?

2. What are some insecure beliefs you have been holding on to that are dragging you into the depths of insecurity with them? Where in your history did these come from?

3. What are more helpful beliefs you can start holding on to as secure anchors during emotional storms to prevent your reactivity?

Chapter Thirteen

The Importance of Repair

Caleb and Ashley have a recurring conflict. Different circumstances set them off, but the core issue is the same. Ashley feels unheard and Caleb feels unfairly criticized. Their pattern for repair (or lack thereof) is consistent: Caleb, an Avoider, will distance, waiting for Ashley to get over it, while Ashley, a Vacillator, will sulk, waiting for Caleb to come and apologize to her. Caleb would try saying sorry at the beginning of their relationship, but Ashley would reject it, telling him if he was *truly* sorry he would stop doing things that hurt her.

Growing up, Ashley had to be the one to apologize for her mom to reengage with her. Her mother would then use Ashley's vulnerability as an opportunity to tell her how "bratty" she'd behaved. She shamed Ashley for her mistakes, telling her, "The best apology is changed behavior."

Caleb and his brother were one year apart. They got along most of the time, but naturally had some sibling rivalry being so close in age. When they did have conflict, instead of finding out what happened, Caleb's dad would tell them, "Blood is thicker than water. You were both wrong. Now shake hands and move on." In Caleb's family, each injured party was expected to move on without real repair, so Caleb gets tired of Ashley holding things over his head.

Avoiders expect others to get over their hurts quickly like they do. "Get over it already" is something they may say or think. Pleasers assume all the blame outwardly, even if they don't believe they should. They apologize because they're afraid of conflict and usually don't get to share their hurt. Vacillators, on the other hand, want the other person to acknowledge first how they believe they've been hurt before they're willing to reengage. They often justify their reactions or are too full of shame to admit they were wrong and apologize. Victims must apologize to Controllers to try and mitigate abuse. And if Controllers apologize, it's usually only as part of the honeymoon period in the cycle of abuse—where the tables temporarily turn—and the Controller is scrambling to manipulate the Victim to not leave, seek help, or tell others about the abuse.

Why You Should Repair

Eventually, both Caleb and Ashley will move on without true resolution. But when repair doesn't happen in a relationship, the pain doesn't just disappear. All the hurt from that incident gets stored and fuels the next conflict. In relationships where both people tend to avoid conflict—like with Avoiders or Pleasers—there may be little visible tension. This can create the illusion that everything is fine, simply because no one is arguing. But as we've explored, the absence of conflict isn't necessarily a sign of a healthy relationship. Conflict, when approached with care, can actually deepen connection. It gives us the chance to see whether others love us enough to forgive us, offer grace, and stay connected despite our flaws—and whether we can do the same. Healthy disagreement allows space to express pain, explore differences, and build trust through honesty. It also helps reveal our blind spots, giving us opportunities to grow. The people who can challenge us with love, who are brave enough to disagree and still stay close, play a unique and essential role in our lives because of this.

While disagreement in itself is not necessarily the enemy, the ways we hurt each other during conflict can put us at odds with one another. If we want secure connection, repair must always follow rupture. Repair is what signals that the relationship can move forward. It doesn't mean all the tension is gone or that both people now see things the same way. It simply means one or both are willing to take responsibility for how their actions caused pain. You can't know someone deeply, let alone go through life with them for years, without occasionally hurting them. And without repair, each unresolved conflict becomes a neural pathway reference point that compounds future offenses. However, when people are able to talk through differences, accept each other's perspectives, and extend forgiveness, it creates a sense of safety in the relationship. If you're seeking secure attachment, the ability to repair, forgive, and offer grace is essential to heal and progress a relationship.

> And without repair, each unresolved conflict becomes a neural pathway reference point that compounds future offenses.

The Benefits of Forgiveness

Forgiveness and grace are closely related, but they aren't the same. Receiving forgiveness means you're released from the punishment you deserve, while grace is getting favor you didn't earn. We have a pillow in our house that has these words sewn into it, "Love me when I least deserve it because that is when I need it most." That's grace—being loved not because of what you've done right, but in spite of what you've done wrong.

Offering forgiveness doesn't mean pretending the offense never happened. It means choosing not to act like the other person continues to owe you for the offense. This is the outward act of forgiveness, which a person may need to perform repeatedly until the feeling of forgiveness follows. Forgiveness starts with an internal reflection where we remind ourselves that because we are not perfect, we also need forgiveness. By forgiving, we acknowledge that we forgive not because others deserve it, but because we don't when we need it.

When we hold onto unforgiveness, this creates bitterness inside us, which fuels feelings of resentment and anger that can eventually lead to contempt for others. This keeps *us* from growing. Resentment is like holding on to receipts of your pain where you remember the price you paid for another's offense against you. Contempt is wanting bad things to happen to the other person. Someone once said, resentment is like drinking poison and expecting the other person to die. But when we can let go of resentment and contempt, we free ourselves. As Lewis B. Smedes, a professor of theology and ethics at Fuller Theological Seminary aptly put it, "To forgive is to set a prisoner free and discover that the prisoner was you."*

> "To forgive is to set a prisoner free and discover that the prisoner was you."

As we choose to forgive, the pain of the transgression can actually decrease. Smedes goes on to say that "forgiving what we cannot forget creates a new way to remember. We change the memory of our past into a hope for our future." In other words, we rewire our brain by forming new neural pathways during the forgiveness process, which allows us to not let the memory of the offense dictate future insecure reactions. Forgiveness is as much—and maybe even more—for the forgiver's benefit as the one being forgiven, as when we create a new way to remember, we take away the power of the offense over us.

Forgiveness Is a Process, Not an Event

Like love and many other emotions, forgiveness is as much an action as it is a feeling. Everett Worthington, a clinical psychologist, has done

---

* Lewis B. Smedes, *Forgive and Forget: Healing the Hurts We Don't Deserve* (HarperOne, 2007).

extensive research on forgiveness. He refers to these two concepts as "decisional forgiveness" and "emotional forgiveness."* While *feeling* like forgiving another person makes granting forgiveness a whole lot easier, *deciding* to forgive first is often what leads to the emotional feeling.

Corrie ten Boom, a Dutch Reformed Christian who, along with her family, hid Jews in her home during the Holocaust, is a great example of this. She and her sister were sent by the Nazis to Ravensbrück concentration camp after it was discovered what they were doing. Corrie watched her sister die in this camp and was released only by chance due to a clerical error. After the war and fueled by her spiritual faith, Corrie travelled Germany preaching forgiveness. After one rally, a former guard at the camp where she was held approached her for forgiveness. He had been particularly cruel to her sister. Corrie described how everything inside of her did not want to forgive *this* man for the brutality he had done to them. However, she overcame her feelings, later writing in her book *The Hiding Place* that she remembered that "forgiveness is an act of the will, and the will can function regardless of the temperature of the heart."**

While many of us may never have to forgive as much cruelty as Corrie was challenged to do, some of us do have deep scars from abuse, abandonment, or hurts suffered. Corrie's example demonstrates it's easier to act your way into a feeling than it is to feel your way into an action. And Worthington has developed a five-step process that has been tested with positive effect in more than twenty controlled studies to help individuals achieve emotional forgiveness. He uses the acronym REACH to remember the steps.

---

*   Everett Worthington, *Forgiveness and Reconciliation: Theory and Application* (Routledge, 2014).
** Corrie ten Boom, with Elizabeth Sherrill and John Sherrill, *The Hiding Place* (Chosen Books, 2008).

- *R* is for "recall"—remembering the hurt that was done to you as objectively as you can.
- *E* is for "empathize"—trying to understand the viewpoint of the person who wronged you.
- *A* is for "altruism"—thinking about a time you hurt someone and were forgiven, then offering the gift of forgiveness to the person who hurt you.
- *C* is for "committing"—publicly forgiving the person who wronged you.
- *H* is for "holding on"—not forgetting the hurt but reminding yourself that you made the choice to forgive.*

The Benefits of Apologizing

Forgiveness is easier when we have an apology, and apologizing is a sign of growth. A person who does not apologize is either not growing or reaching perfection! It may be true that as we grow, we learn to not make the same mistakes as often, so naturally, we would have less of those infractions to apologize for; however, growth also involves gaining insight and awareness of the ways our actions impact others. So, as we grow, we will become more aware of the ways we hurt others where we need forgiveness.

Our ability to forgive others is correlated to our ability to show humility and ask for forgiveness, and apologizing for an offense can help an offended party to offer us forgiveness. Worthington notes, "Research reveals that the difficulty of forgiving is directly related to the size of the injustice gap." This gap can be reduced when we offer sincere apologies or make amends that "restore some sense of justice to thinking about the offense" for the offended person. So, apologizing for our mistakes

---

* Everett Worthington, "Research," personal website, http://www.evworthington-forgiveness.com/research.

helps others forgive *us*, as well as helping *us* offer forgiveness to others when they need it.

How Not to Apologize

Giving an apology is an act of courage; you're making yourself vulnerable and showing humility by admitting a fault and acknowledging an area you need to grow in. True remorse comes from the guilt we feel by way of cognitive dissonance—acting in opposition to our values. However, when apologies follow from a feeling of shame, we are more likely to self-protect at the same time by blaming, justifying, or minimizing to try and reduce our shame. Here are what apologies driven by shame look like:

- *"I'm sorry, but you should not have…"* [Blame]
- *"I'm sorry, but I had to do that because…"* [Justification]
- *"I'm sorry but it's not as bad as you are making it out to be."* [Minimization]

When we use a "but," this does not show humility and is not a sincere apology. Neither is apologizing for someone else's feelings: "I'm sorry you feel that way." This often communicates you wish they agreed with you. These apologies are usually not received well because they are disingenuous, unempathetic, or communicate that the other person is wrong for feeling the way they do. People don't choose their emotions; it's simply how they feel in that moment and that's not necessarily wrong in itself.

> Giving an apology is an act of courage.

There's an important difference between apologizing out of remorse and apologizing out of shame. Remorse focuses on the other person's pain of what they went through. Shame, on the other hand, centers on your own pain about how bad you feel. And when you have the type of chronic shame where you self-deprecate, you steal that person's moment for relief because they must now comfort you to help you recover. You might think you're taking greater ownership by doing this, but the other person may feel guilty for expressing their pain because you feel so bad. The goal of an apology is to soothe a wound, and when we apologize with self-protective shame strategies, these have the opposite effect.

How to Apologize for True Repair and Forgiveness

True apologies show accountability, remorse, and an understanding of how you hurt the other person. Here are the five "*A*'s" to giving an effective apology:

1. Admit what you did that was wrong: *"I'm sorry that I got angry and (did what I did)."*
2. Ask how your actions impacted them: *"How did you feel when I did that?"*
3. Acknowledge their feelings by validating and/or empathizing: *"I can see how when I did that you felt (emotion they expressed). It makes sense why you distanced from me."* [Validation] *"It must be difficult to know what to do when I act like that."* [Empathy]
4. Amend if necessary: *"I want to fix what I broke. It was wrong of me."*
5. Accountability: *"I will commit to doing better in the future, and here's how I plan on doing that…"*

Showing Grace (Even When You're Not Wrong)

It can also be appropriate to seek repair (notice I did not say apologize) even when we haven't done anything objectively wrong. People can have perceived offenses, especially in our modern-day culture, feeling hurt by something we say or do (or don't say or do), even if no harm was intended. In these moments, especially when we believe we've acted appropriately, it can be powerful and gracious to acknowledge the other person's feelings and express empathy for their hurt. Even when someone's emotions are exaggerated by past wounds we were not at fault for, genuine empathy can create an opportunity for their healing and create connection.

Being secure in yourself means you know recognizing someone's feelings and perceived hurts is not assuming fault. You can honor their emotions and still maintain the right to believe you did nothing wrong. Try saying something like *"I am sad you feel hurt by that,"* or *"I see [describe action or circumstance] hurt you—that wasn't my intention."* This allows you to connect in a relational way without expressly apologizing or compromising your beliefs.

You might also make a commitment to not say or do certain things around someone in personal settings, as much as it is reasonably possible, if you know it may cause them distress. There's a difference between intentionally avoiding certain topics in shared, respectful spaces—like a family gathering or when spending time with a friend—where you know they may take offense, and expressing your views in public forums, such as on social media, where others can limit their exposure or choose to remove themselves.

You also have the right to uphold your own boundaries, including your right to express yourself freely. If someone chooses to bring up a topic, they should expect others might share their perspectives as well. That said, deliberately bringing up a topic just to provoke someone, especially when you know it's unlikely to lead to a productive conversation, is inconsiderate and unkind.

When faced with a circumstance where another person is offended by something you don't see as an infraction, you can follow these steps for repair:

1. Listen to how your actions impacted the other person
2. Acknowledge their feelings
3. Validate or empathize with the other person's pain
4. Make a commitment to be as considerate of them in the future as *reasonably* possible.

Responding Well to an Apology

There is an art to receiving an apology well. Don't brush it off with phrases like "Don't worry about it," or "It's fine." Remember, offering an apology takes courage and vulnerability. Honor that moment by acknowledging the person's humility and responding with grace. This is your opportunity to talk about your pain as a way to help close the injustice gap for your internal healing and reduce any triggers you have or that could form. However, don't use moments of other's vulnerability as an opportunity to admonish them while their guard is down, or as a discipline moment with children if you are angry. Some good initial responses to an apology would be:

- *"Thank you."*
- *"I appreciate that."*
- *"That means a lot to me."*

It's important to recognize that forgiveness and reconciliation are two different things. While offering forgiveness is as much for your benefit and *necessary* for healthy reconciliation, it does not mean forgiveness should always lead to reconciliation. It may not be safe or wise for you to reconcile with a person who is dangerous or has harmed your well-being in a serious way, or if they show no recognition of or remorse for the damage they've caused. If someone's actions are truly destructive, reconciliation should be dependent upon a genuine commitment to changed behavior. Without that, reconciliation may only open the door to more harm. Forgiveness also still allows for consequences, which may be the most loving thing to do to keep you or others safe, or for the offender to take responsibility for their actions.

Choosing not to reconcile should be given serious thought and not used as an excuse to avoid or detach because you find it uncomfortable to face working out differences or grow into security. Work with a professional if you think you are being emotionally abused.

> Forgiveness and reconciliation are two different things.

A therapist can help you discern whether what you are experiencing is truly abusive or if you may be contributing to a negative cycle that needs attention from both sides. That said, if several trusted people in your life are expressing concern for your well-being and encouraging you to detach from someone, take this seriously. A therapist can support you in how to safely break away from someone if needed.

While learning to walk the path of authentic forgiveness and grace is challenging, healing and restoration is waiting for you as you do this. Like all the growth steps in this section, forgiveness must be practiced for you to get better at it. Forgiveness must also be freely given. It cannot be earned, for if it is, then it is not forgiveness at all because the debt has been paid.

To turn such difficult practices into new habits, it can help to continually remind yourself that you're gaining experience and stamina in this, and not expected to have perfect success every time. To stay encouraged, you'll need to be aware of some common barriers that frequently impede progress. Let's move on to our final chapter and look at those.

REFLECT

1. What were the lessons from your family-of-origin on repair and forgiveness?

2. Did you have a parent who apologized to you when they were wrong, or you were harmed? Was it a full apology with the Five *A*'s? If, not, which ones were missing and how did that affect your relationship with them?

3. Who do you need to apologize to and who do you need to forgive?

4. Which parts of the apology process do you find most challenging or need to improve in?

5. In what areas of the forgiveness process could you improve or deepen your understanding?

Chapter Fourteen

Measuring Progress and Avoiding Pitfalls

So yesterday I told Jake it was time to stop playing his video game and he got frustrated like always and screamed at me that it wasn't fair, and I never give him enough time."

Sherrie shifted to sit further back on the couch, and I thought I detected a difference in her tone from last time. She looked back at me with determination. "But I finally did something different. Instead of getting activated and totally losing it at his disrespect, I stopped to take a few deep breaths and manage my anxiety. I thought about what you told me: *Help him with words for his feelings.* So, I said, 'I know you feel disappointed, when time's up. I'm willing to listen to how you feel about that if you can come to me and speak without blaming or getting so loud.'"

"Wow. Well done!" I said, remembering our discussion last week about diffusing her son's protests.

"He did come to me, and I said, 'If you tell me your feelings, I'll try and empathize with you, even if I disagree with giving you what you want.' He was so surprised I didn't yell back. And he backed down and agreed he was disappointed. We had a short conversation that it was okay for him to feel disappointed and that he did not have to agree with me either, but I did expect him to be respectful in his responses, as I would also be respectful to him in mine. It felt *so good* to handle that so calmly!"

"That's amazing, Sherrie. I'm so proud of you!"

Sherrie felt good about being in control of her emotions rather than letting them control her, so she could put into practice one of her growth goals. She was finally enjoying some progress because of her commitment to growth.

Building Your Coherent Narrative

You've made it to the home stretch! Let's recap what we have covered so far. We've examined:

- How attachment forms
- The childhood stages of development and how the Comfort Circle can help conversations through reparative experiences of the cycle of bonding
- The amygdala's role in reactivity to perceived threats
- How we develop self-protective strategies that become habitual reactions
- How shame holds us back from growth and how to overcome it
- How each insecure attachment style reacts to relational distress
- The growth goals for each style to work toward greater security
- The common barriers that form our resistance to growth
- The role of brain associations on beliefs we form
- The importance of forgiveness for relational repair and personal healing

From all this, I hope you have a framework for your personal coherent narrative and a plan for how to earn secure attachment through working on your growth goals. Remember, it's not how difficult your childhood was that determines if you can earn secure attachment, it's how you can make sense of what happened to you.

My friend Kay Yerkovich says growth is a small miracle, meaning it's a gradual progress that takes place over time as our efforts build momentum. Building your coherent narrative should be an ongoing process that happens through continued examination, awareness, and practice in the above areas. Whatever you practice you get better at because it's neural pathway-building. So, when you keep repeating what you've learned, you will grow. In this final chapter, I want to look at how to measure your progress and note some final pitfalls to avoid.

> It's not how difficult your childhood was that determines if you can earn secure attachment, it's how you can make sense of what happened to you.

Measuring Growth

We can't switch on desirable behaviors and off undesirable ones like a light switch. Growth takes time. When I used to work with children with severe attachment behaviors, a former clinical supervisor of mine gave me a great picture of growth I was able to share with parents. She took out a piece of paper and drew the following:

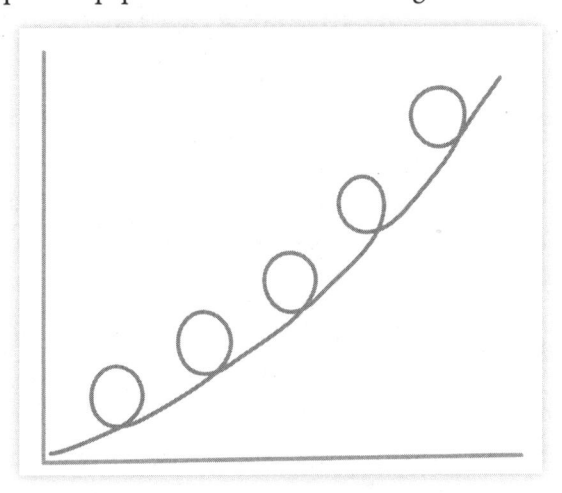

She was emphasizing the point that growth is not linear. We are human and so we stumble. Relapse is often a stage in recovery because old neural pathways are hard to break, and it's easy to slip back into them. But this doesn't mean we're not progressing. Instead, progress should be measured by *frequency*, *intensity*, and *duration*. Though it may not feel like it, if you have two outbursts in a week when you used to have five, you're making progress! If you still yell at others but no longer swear, you're making progress! And if your outburst lasted only ten minutes when it used to be twenty or longer, you're making progress! Not being where you want to be yet does not mean you are not moving forward. In this chapter, I want to address ways you can better track your growth and anticipate the ways you might stall so you don't get stuck in hopelessness.

> Relapse is often a stage in recovery.

Recover, Repair, and Reconnect

Another great way to measure growth in a relationship is by how quickly you can recover, repair, and reconnect after a conflict happens.

- **Recover**—How quickly can you reset, either after making a mistake or after another person has offended you?
- **Repair**—How quickly can you move to resolving a conflict, and asking for or granting forgiveness, even if you're still hurt or they aren't initiating?
- **Reconnect**—How quickly can you get back to being connected by owning your part in a relational rupture, even if you're not entirely at fault?

Repair should always follow a relational rupture. Without it, the hurt gets stored and your resentment piles up, only to fuel your reactivity in the next conflict. So learning to repair effectively is essential to your growth.

Developing Your Observing Self

Each of the insecure attachment styles shares this growth goal of developing the observing self. At the start of follow-up therapy sessions, I like to ask, "So what did you notice about yourself this week?" I know individuals are making progress when they're gaining new insight from self-reflection between sessions, and have examples of the practice work they've been doing to lean into their areas of growth. As you develop your observing self and reflect on your behaviors to understand the emotions driving them, you will gain these new insights too. People who do this find it's not uncommon to gain new insights weekly. And because it's so important, let's review the four questions to develop this observing self:

1. What am I *feeling*?
2. What is *happening* around me right now, or what just happened?
3. How am I *reacting* to get the corresponding need met or to manage my need not getting met?
4. When in my history did I have similar associations and *learn* that reaction?

Never Waste a Good Conflict

A secure response is less about what's right or wrong, and more about responding versus reacting. We can't control all situations or what others do or don't do. But we can learn to better manage our responses. A good magician uses the art of misdirection to divert your focus while his sleight of hand tricks you into believing what he wants you to. When people are so focused on convincing you of who or what is right or wrong, they'll often get misdirected from seeing their ingrained, insecure reactions and learning a better response, which can be given regardless of who's right or wrong.

I often tell people, never waste a good conflict! Progress happens when you can deconstruct a relational rupture and see what you can learn. How could things have gone differently? What might you have done to manage your emotions and reactions better? With couples, once they see where situations took a turn for the worse and caused the rupture, hindsight becomes the tool to determine together what they can do differently the next time, rather than staying stuck focusing on who was right or wrong. Once you can see your core conflict pattern, you can learn to predict it. Only then will you have the know-how to overcome it.

> Once you can see your core conflict pattern, you can learn it to predict it.

Often, we need to choose between being "right" and progressing our relationships. You might be right, but if your words and actions aren't doing good, you're not gaining ground in your relationship. Being right and doing good are not always the same thing. Our moral sense of justice and rightness or wrongness loves to debate, but we have trouble listening and really hearing each other when we're geared up to fight. When you strongly disagree with someone, try not to correct facts, but instead hear, acknowledge, and empathize with their pain. Connection happens when we understand one another. You can't understand someone if you're at the same time trying to get them to see things a different way. And it's possible to still connect and hold others accountable in a secure way, even when you disagree.

Mislabeled and Misplaced Emotions

Sometimes people mislabel their emotions or they're misplaced, which causes them to seek the wrong need. This can lead to confusion and misunderstanding.

Sally and Jim showed up at one session visibly upset at each other. Sally felt offended by Jim's lack of table manners when they went out to dinner with her boss and his wife. To Sally, Jim made several social faux pas during the meal, like having his elbows on the table and taking the last bread roll without asking if anyone else wanted it. Teaching and enforcing manners had been an important value to Sally's parents, and they taught her that not demonstrating good manners was a sign of disrespect. Often, they'd used shame tactics, and Sally became a rule follower. Jim hadn't intended to offend, so both were frustrated, with Sally trying to convince Jim of his disrespect, and Jim defending his innocence.

It may seem small, but many people feel disrespected when others don't clean up after themselves, arrive on time, or adhere to some other value that was given great importance in their childhood homes. While such situations should elicit feelings of being unseen, unconsidered, or disappointed, often these individuals grew up in homes where they were told it was disrespectful to leave a mess or show up late, intentional or not. Because respect is the corresponding need for disrespect, if this feeling is misplaced then a misplaced need is sought, and the other person might have a hard time admitting they were being disrespectful by unintentionally making a mistake or not sharing a value.

If others seem confused about the emotion you are expressing from a situation, ask yourself: *"Does it make sense to feel this emotion in this circumstance?"* There may not really be disrespect, or rejection, or any bad intention at all, behind the actions, even if you feel that way. The misplaced emotion is often the key back into the childhood wound for coherent narrative building.

If, before accusing Jim, Sally had been able to take some time to reflect and notice when she had first felt this way in a similar situation, she could have made the connection to her past. Jim would've been more open to understanding her feelings and they could have talked productively about why it upset her so much and how to manage future situations.

Listener Guidelines

As a listener, your role isn't to judge, fix, or argue—it's to understand. Recognize that the speaker has just as much right to their perspective as you do to yours. Rather than evaluating their words as right or wrong, remind yourself: *"I can listen fully without needing to agree."*

> *"I can listen fully without needing to agree."*

Let go of the urge to interrupt, correct, or shift the conversation toward your point of view. And avoid defending yourself, explaining your intentions, or minimizing what the other person feels. Listening means holding space for the other—not rushing to offer your side or to "set the record straight."

When it's your turn to speak, you'll have the opportunity to share your experience. But until then, try not to defend, deny, blame, minimize, distract, pacify, or fix. These often leave the speaker feeling dismissed or misunderstood—and when someone doesn't feel heard, they're far less likely to listen to you after.

Even if what the speaker shares is difficult to hear—especially if it's a negative opinion about you—practice staying present. You can acknowledge their perspective even if you don't intend to adopt it. You might say, *"Can you help me understand what led you to feel that way?"* This opens dialogue without resistance or reactivity.

Use "You" reflections to summarize what they said if you believe you are not to blame, so you can repeat without invalidating what they said. *"I understand you felt..."* or *"You saw..."* or *"You experienced..."* When you show you're trying to listen and understand them, others have less of a need to be defensive and are more likely to feel valued. You can listen well and still maintain your own perspective if it differs, if you remember: The goal of listening is understanding, not agreement.

Speaker Guidelines

As the speaker, aim for connection—not control. Speak in short, digestible statements rather than long explanations or lectures. This gives your listener space to reflect, connect, and respond without feeling overwhelmed.

Avoid blame or accusation. "You" statements as a speaker often trigger defensiveness and shut down open communication. Instead, use "I" statements to express your internal experience: *"I felt…"* or *"I saw…"* or *"I heard…"* or *"I experienced…"*

This language keeps the focus on your perspective, making it easier for others to hear and validate your emotions, even if they don't fully agree with your point of view.

When sharing, speak from the heart—not just from the facts or your perceived offenses. "I feel" statements should name real emotions (like confusion, disappointment, hurt, or fear), not thoughts or assumptions. For example, avoid *"I feel like you're abandoning me."* That usually leads to judgment rather than vulnerability. Instead try, "I feel abandoned when…" One opens the door for empathy; the other often closes it.

After sharing your emotions, don't just ask for changed behavior, but make the link to the corresponding need: *"I feel worried and need reassurance,"* or *"I feel sad and need comfort."* This is what will help you truly feel resolved, and the other person might be able to think of ways to provide this need for you other than how you initially think they should. Be clear about what you want from others, and let them decide whether or how they can provide this. Don't assume they should know your need or how they must respond. People may not respond how you hope—and while that can hurt, it doesn't mean your feelings aren't valid or they don't recognize those feelings or empathize with you. They're

> Don't assume they should know your need or how they must respond.

responsible for their responses, just as you are responsible for your emotional world.

And that brings us to ownership. Take full ownership of your feelings rather than blaming the other person for causing them and expecting them to adjust so you feel better. Remember what Dr. Bruce Banner says, right before he turns into the Incredible Hulk?

"Don't make me angry, you won't like me when I'm angry!"

The implication is he can't be held responsible for his anger or reactions, because others are the cause of his feelings. Many of us unintentionally place our emotions in someone else's hands too:

- *"You make me so mad."*
- *"You're stressing me out."*
- *"You hurt my feelings."*

These may feel true in the moment, but when we frame our emotions as something others cause, we also make them responsible for healing us or for our reactions—and that's not fair or sustainable. It's like giving someone a remote control to your nervous system. That's too much power to give someone over you. Remember, often our feelings in the present are driven by past wounds that the other person is not responsible for. And many times our wounds are triggered unintentionally by the other.

Instead, try:

- *"I feel angry when this happens."*
- *"I feel anxious when I don't hear from you."*

The difference is subtle, but powerful. The more responsibility you take for your emotional experience, the more freedom and peace you'll have, and the more engagement you'll get from the listener. Because unless you master your emotional state, your emotional state will master you. And you can only master the emotions you own.

When you squeeze a tube, what comes out? Whatever's inside. So, when someone squeezes you, notice what comes out. If you don't like it, you're the only one who can change it.

Being Responsible For vs. Having Responsibility To

This is a nuanced and challenging concept to grasp, but is essential for overcoming a common and significant pitfall. If you don't fully grasp the difference at first, you may need to read this more than once. For when you comprehend this deeper understanding, you will discover a freedom that can transform how you relate to yourself and others. We are each *responsible for* ourselves, yet also *responsible to* others—a distinction that is so often misunderstood. Being *responsible for* means taking ownership and accountability for your own actions and the consequences they bring, with the goal of fostering personal growth. Being *responsible to* means maintaining a healthy attitude and making thoughtful decisions in your relationship with another person, to encourage their growth without trying to control it.

Avoiders tend to overemphasize independence, with each individual having *responsibility for* self above all else, seeing little *responsibility to* help others. In contrast, Pleasers and Victims give too much *responsibility to* managing others' emotions, while neglecting *responsibility for* standing up for themselves. Meanwhile, Vacillators and Controllers may, at different times, avoid taking *responsibility for* their reactions by justifying them, while also neglecting their *responsibility to* others by using protests and manipulation.

While we should not take *responsibility for* another adult's actions, we can be *responsible to* help them grow. Children start life with a blank slate, so as parents we have both a *responsibility for* them until they can make their own choices and also a *responsibility to* teach them to make healthy choices. Primarily, teaching happens through modeling of behaviors, and as they gain understanding of consequences, our *responsibility for* them reduces. Yet, as they grow and become independent to make their own age-appropriate choices, our *responsibility to* keep modeling good behavior remains. We teach them how to choose and what to consider, but they must ultimately take *responsibility for* themselves if they are to grow into maturity and security.

In adult relationships, this principle matters just as much, though adult-to-adult is very different from parent-to-child. Yes, each of us is *responsible for* managing our own emotions and actions—but we also hold a *responsibility to* others to resolve conflict in an emotionally secure way. Think about this: When you're upset, do you want someone to simply say, *"That's your problem. Deal with it"*? Or do you hope they'll listen, acknowledge your pain, and partner with you to find some resolution—even if they don't agree with everything you think?

And when you want them to take accountability, that's not just because you think it's "right," but also because it would help you heal and feel heard. That's the impact of being *responsible to* someone. While we can't control each other's speed of growth, we can profoundly influence it through the way we show up for one another. When two people in conflict believe the other person is to blame and solely responsible to repair the relationship, they remain stuck.

Now, this doesn't mean you have to tolerate ongoing harm or "just get over it." Growth and healing often require boundaries. Part of being *responsible for* yourself is learning when to say, *"This isn't okay,"* until the other person is ready to take ownership of their own behavior.

But what if letting go of your anger isn't about excusing the hurt—but about freeing yourself from the burden of carrying it? **The surprising benefit of releasing emotional reactivity is that you don't have to be reactive anymore!** Then you're more capable of being *responsible to* others in a fuller way and making yourself available for restoration and secure connection.

This is the transformative part of growth. As you take more *responsibility for* your healing, you naturally become more *responsible to* the people around you. And that's where real connection begins. This is a difficult teaching for many because so often our reactivity feels justified. But consider this: Your future, healed self—the one who feels secure and grounded—may see things in a way you can't yet imagine. So, keep growing. The secure version of you you're becoming will thank you.

Stop Wishing and Start Hoping

Wishing and hoping may seem similar, but they come from very different places. Hope is grounded in reality; it's the belief that a desired outcome is possible, supported by some evidence or reason to believe it could happen. Wishing, on the other hand, is idealizing. It often reflects a longing for something that's unlikely or even impossible, and it's usually driven by subconscious expectations.

We all carry expectations of others, and expectations, in themselves, aren't bad. But idealized expectations—those not rooted in current reality—set us up for deeper disappointment. If what we expect from a person or situation isn't based on consistent behavior or recent evidence, it's not hope we're holding onto. It's a wish.

Wishing creates an internal longing for things to turn out a certain way. It's often tied to thoughts like *"I wish they were more attentive."* These aren't grounded in what is, but in what we imagine should be. And when reality doesn't align with that imagined ideal, we're left feeling let down, agitated, and sometimes even crushed.

Sometimes idealization occurs after the outcome of an event when we are stuck on wishing someone had not done something or something had not happened. A good guide to assess whether your expectations are idealizations is: If you have a minor sense of disappointment that you can recover from, you had an expectation; if you have a great sense of disappointment that you can't easily recover from, usually demonstrated by reactivity out of proportion to the event, you were likely idealizing. Though every insecure attachment style can idealize at times, Vacillators, in particular, tend to do so the most with people and relationships, and end up feeling very let down, resulting in them feeling hopeless.

True hope allows for disappointment, and even anticipates it, without falling apart. It accepts that things might not turn out how we want, and grants room for growth. It equips us to learn from outcomes and adjust our expectations going forward. Disappointment is normal. Everyone feels it. But how we respond to it reveals whether we're caught in idealization or grounded in acceptance.

We can't always avoid being let down, but we can work on our expectations and learn to recover quicker. Here's a small personal example: Years ago, my wife accidentally dinged my car door. It was a minor thing, an accident, and I knew that. It happened when she was doing me a favor. But every time I saw the ding, part of me still wished she'd been more careful. Whenever I caught myself wishing this hadn't happened, I remembered that wishing wouldn't change that, and only kept me stuck in disappointment. So, I decided to let it go. It wasn't easy, and it took time. I had to practice acceptance every time it came to mind, and eventually it didn't bother me any longer.

> Wishing looks backward with longing, while hope looks forward with acceptance.

I don't always get it right, but the truth I hold onto is: Wishing looks backward with longing, while hope looks forward with acceptance.

Wishes only come true in fairytales. And in the end, it's always better to work through disappointment than to get stuck wishing for a different outcome to the story.

Focus on Patterns, Not Problems

In graduate school, I worked as a buyer for a major car dealership chain. When we suspected a vehicle might have an engine or transmission problem, we would "put the pedal to the metal" during the test drive phase of the vehicle inspection. When an engine and transmission are under pressure, underlying problems are accentuated and easier to notice. Humans are the same. While having less conflict can be an indicator of growth, the measure of your growth is made evident by how you handle stressful situations when you are put under pressure.

Some people initiate therapy only once they have a crisis, and then decide whether to come each week based on the level of distress they're feeling about it. These individuals tend to have limited insight into the patterns that got them into the crisis. And once their symptoms ease, they stop coming. Doing therapy when you're *not* in crisis is often when you can make the most progress. With the presenting problem out of the way, growth goals appear less overwhelming. Many times, I hear back from the clients that drop out prematurely once their distress becomes unmanageable again. Had they simply stayed in therapy to work though their insecurities, they could have conquered the patterns that keep them getting stuck.

Practice in Real Time

Other times progress is limited when clients are not as actively involved in the earned security process. I usually notice this more in couples therapy when one spouse is more committed to coming than the other. When I ask about their practice between sessions, the noncommittal person tends to say, *"I had a busy week and I didn't have much time to review the materials or practice the skills."* But growth doesn't take more time, it takes more *intention*.

One of the first basic needs children learn to meet is to feed themselves. Learning to take responsibility to feed yourself is a sign of growth and maturity. If you're not growing and your relationships are staying stuck because you continue to say you don't have time, you may be expecting someone else to feed you.

You can use attentive, active, and reflective listening skills with customers, colleagues, friends, and family in everyday interactions. You can decide to listen first in a conversation and do so without defensiveness when you disagree with what's said, or commit to not to fixing others' problems or managing their emotions when they are distressed. When you speak, you can do so without criticizing or blaming, and choose to verbalize your emotions and needs in a healthy way. You can accept displeasure from others while holding healthy boundaries, create space to calm down in conflict and not react, and use your alone time to reflect on thoughts, emotions, and behaviors. Even just notice what bubbles up when someone says something you disagree with, or when someone cuts you off in traffic, or when you're waiting in a slow-moving line. Opportunities to practice come without creating any "extra" time. Though it could be if you spent less time on your phone or watching TV you would have more time for intentional conversations.

One client, who was learning to put on her observing self, told me it was like she began hearing a new internal voice speaking to her about her interactions. When you practice putting on your observing self, and start to make the subconscious *conscious*, you will notice a lot more happening inside you than you once realized.

Other Common Objections

If you've lost that loving feeling or don't feel like doing it, remember, acts of love can help bring back the feelings of love. You don't expect any of your other emotions you're not feeling at this moment to never come back again, do you? Emotions come and go, and the fact that you used to "feel like it" means you're capable of feeling it again!

For others, the objection is more principled: *"Too much hurt has happened between us to heal and forgive."* Yet consider if there's a type of hopelessness there or unwillingness to forgive. When author C. S. Lewis faced this realization that he was refusing to forgive, he wrote, "But years later it occurred to me that there was one man to whom I had been [separating the actions from the actor] all my life—namely myself. However much I might dislike my own cowardice or conceit or greed, I went on loving myself. There had never been the slightest difficulty about it."* What loving parent doesn't separate their child from their mistakes and continue loving and forgiving them? When others are willing to change and grow, we do well to grant forgiveness, not because they deserve it, but because we also don't. And once you do you might be surprised how your thoughts and feelings can change.

Your Desire vs. Your Defiance

One final encouragement: As a bloke from England, I watch a lot of soccer (football to the locals). I frequently enjoy the post-match analysis after the game, and whenever the games are close, the former players with long experience will comment on the winning team's mentality of having great "desire" to win, or the underdog team's remarkable "defiance" in holding off the attacks.

Similarly, the difference between people who succeed in earning secure attachment versus those who stay stuck in their insecurities comes down to this. Your desire to earn security must be greater than your defiance against your insecurities being broken down. Those with the strong desire to unshackle themselves from their insecure attachment

---

* C. S. Lewis, *Mere Christianity* (Dolphin, 1969).

style will push through any challenge, recover from mistakes, recognize and admit their shame, and lean into discomfort for the reward of growth. Yet those who are defiant in their insecure attachment impulses will be mastered by their shame, will be unwilling to listen when they disagree, may be aggressive or avoidant in sharing their feelings, and will stay focused on the behaviors of others to determine their happiness.

Here, I am reminded of the Native American "Legend of Two Wolves." The story goes that an elder once taught his grandson about a battle that goes on inside each of us. These are two wolves, he said, one good and the other evil. The boy thought for a moment and then asked, "But which wolf wins?" And the grandfather answered, "The one that you feed." It's a simple idea, but one of great wisdom. **You don't get to choose <u>whether</u> you practice, but you do get to choose <u>what</u> you practice. And whatever you practice you *will* reinforce.** Every situation is another opportunity to take responsibility and make your future easier. To build a new adaptive neural pathway, or to reinforce the existing insecure one. The growth you will experience directly correlates to the amount of discomfort you're willing to endure. You either take control of your attachment style, or it will continue to have control over you. The choice is yours: Which attachment style will you feed?

> You either take control of your attachment style, or it will continue to have control over you.

A Final Note: Hold On to Hope!

I've been working with Amber for several years now. When we first met, she was a deeply anxious Pleaser. She battled depression and anxiety that affected her self-esteem, made social interactions overwhelming, and filled her with an intense fear of judgment and intrusive thoughts. Over the years, she's tried various medications with mixed results. But she's persevered, and month by month, she's made steady, meaningful progress.

Recently, Amber became a mother, and it's further fueled her motivation to break the cycle of anxiety and create a healthier emotional legacy. It had been a couple of months since I had seen her, but at our latest session, she walked in with confidence, making strong eye contact, and carrying a story that moved us both.

Her parents had given her a box of childhood keepsakes, and inside, she discovered a journal she'd written when she was just nine years old. Reading through the pages, she was struck by how early her anxiety had taken root. She wrote about worries over her parents fighting, being responsible for her younger siblings, and even fears about the national debt that she'd seen the president talking about on TV—concerns far beyond what a child should bear. One entry especially stood out: a fear of riding in the car with her grandmother. "I'm so scared of her driving and that we're going to crash and die," it read. Amber had long forgotten this memory, but the resemblance to the intrusive driving-related thoughts she's experienced in recent years was undeniable.

Though hard to read, she described finding the journal as "a mercy." It gave her the ability to connect the dots and link her present fears to early, formative experiences. Since then, she told me she's made significant strides in challenging her thoughts, reshaping beliefs, and responding with emotional security rather than fear. She's been developing her observing self, and the journal gave her a missing piece of the puzzle, helping her create a more coherent and compassionate narrative about who she is now and how she got here.

I'm incredibly proud of Amber. Her growth hasn't come easy. It's taken grit, resilience, and the willingness to confront hard things. But she's living proof that putting in the work, while not without struggle, is so worth it! Her courage and desire to overcome her insecurities is inspiring and has helped her hold on to hope. And as you begin to see the exciting results of your efforts, I believe your own growth will do the same for you.

REFLECT

1. How quickly can you recover, repair, and reconnect?

2. Can you separate your thoughts from your feelings and communicate each of these accurately?

3. Which pitfalls or objections you read about in this chapter keep you stuck?

4. Is your desire to earn secure attachment greater than your insecure attachment style defiance to not grow?

Appendix
Needs for Emotions Chart

Emotion	Need
Anger / Aggravated / Irritated	Soothed (through seeing hurt, sad, or fear)
Anxious / Nervous / Worry / Embarrassed	Reassurance
Pain / Hurt / Injured	Relief / Comfort / Healing
Guilt / Shame / Exposed / Remorse / Rejected	Acceptance / Forgiveness / Inclusion
Fear / Scared / Afraid / Insecure	Security / Protection / Safety
Lonely / Abandoned / Isolated	Companionship / Connection
Sad / Upset / Miserable / Heartbroken	Comfort
Overwhelmed / Annoyed / Frustrated	Solution / Distraction (break) / Peace
Flustered	Reassurance
Stressed / Preoccupied / Distracted	Calm / Focus
Controlled / Restricted	Freedom / Cooperation / Autonomy / Independence / Choice / Space
Confused / Torn / Ambivalent	Clarity / Certainty
Chaotic / Disorganized / Out of Control	Peace / Structure / Order / Harmony / Stability / Consistency
Guarded / Hesitant / Wary / Apprehensive / Suspicious / Cautious	Trust / Safety
Unloved	Love / Acceptance / Belonging
Unheard	Heard / Listened to / Views Considered

Unseen / Unimportant / Overlooked / Invisible / Forgotten	Seen / Prioritized / Recognized / Acknowledged / Noticed
Hopeless / Despair	Hope
Helpless / Distressed	Help / Security / Support
Betrayed / Mistrust	Trust / Integrity / Honesty
Misunderstood	Understanding
Disconnected	Connection
Disrespected	Respect
Disappointed / Discouraged / Disheartened	Encouragement
Unstable / Unsupported	Stability / Support
Inconsistent	Consistency
Tense	Relax
Bored / Indifferent	Challenge
Cheated	Fairness / Justice
Restless / Impatient	Let energy out
Disgusted / Resentful / Jealous / Envious	Understanding
Vulnerable / Sensitive / Self-Conscious / Embarrassed / Uncomfortable / Insecure	Sensitivity / Acceptance / Security
Depressed	Companionship / Understanding / Compassion
Tired / Lethargic / Worn out	Rest / Calm / Peace

The Cycle of How We Try to Get Our Needs Met

Behaviors

Behaviors are driven by emotions and feelings trying to get a need met.

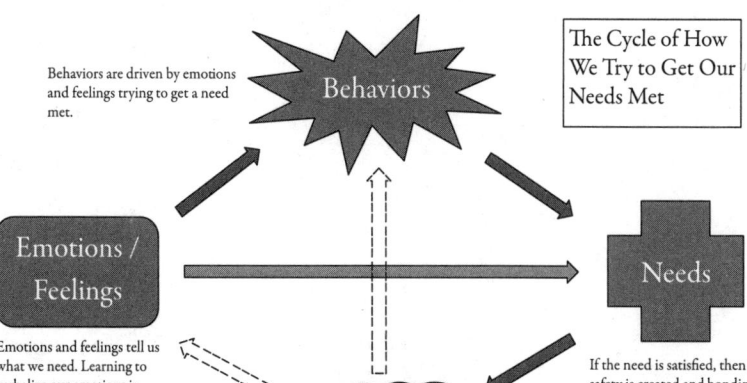

Emotions / Feelings

Emotions and feelings tell us what we need. Learning to verbalize our emotions in secure ways and ask for our needs reduces some of the need to act them out for others to understand them.

Needs

If the need is satisfied, then safety is created and bonding occurs. If not, then a coping strategy is formed (limited expression of emotions, anxiety to please others so as to mitigate potential threats, anger and pouting for others to notice our needs are not being attended to, withdrawal to protect oneself from further harm, or fighting back to stop from being controlled).

Thoughts

Satisfied or unsatisfied needs fuel thoughts about how future behaviors can get needs met and either result in positive feelings from the need being met or drive despair over unmet needs and the likelihood of them continuing to not be met in the future. Beliefs are then formed about ourselves from repeated or significant experiences. (Example: "I am seen, known, loved, and important, and my needs can get met", or "I am not seen, known, loved, or important, and it's hopeless for my needs to get met" or "I need to do [XYZ] in order to get my needs met.")

©Marc Cameron 2025

Answer with: (H) Habitually (>80%) (O) Often (50–79%) (S) Sometimes (20–49%) (R) Rarely (5–19%) (N) Not that I could notice (<5% of the time)

Mother = ◯   Father = /   Example (H) (O) (S̸) (R) (Ⓝ)

Attachment Assessment

1. My mother/father told me "I love you." (H) (O) (S) (R) (N)
2. My mother/father hugged, kissed, and touched me in ways so I felt loved. (H) (O) (S) (R) (N)
3. My mother/father acknowledged and talked to me about my emotions. (H) (O) (S) (R) (N)
4. My mother/father understood the ways I acted when I was hurt or stressed. (H) (O) (S) (R) (N)
5. My mother/father comforted me when I was sad or hurting. (H) (O) (S) (R) (N)
6. My mother/father allowed me to express anger and negative emotions. (H) (O) (S) (R) (N)
7. My mother/father responded to my emotions with empathy and validation. (H) (O) (S) (R) (N)
8. My mother/father modeled for me and taught me how to navigate conflict. (H) (O) (S) (R) (N)
9. My mother/father disciplined me to teach life lessons rather than punitively. (H) (O) (S) (R) (N)
10. My mother/father offered me forgiveness and grace. (H) (O) (S) (R) (N)
11. My mother/father allowed me to have a "do over" when I made a mistake. (H) (O) (S) (R) (N)
12. My mother/father apologized to me when they wronged me. (H) (O) (S) (R) (N)
13. My mother/father made me feel safe. (H) (O) (S) (R) (N)
14. My mother/father allowed me to have privacy and space to individuate. (H) (O) (S) (R) (N)
15. My mother/father spent time with me doing the things I liked to do. (H) (O) (S) (R) (N)
16. My mother/father laughed with me. (H) (O) (S) (R) (N)

17. My mother/father spent time listening to me and hearing my requests. (H) (O) (S) (R) (N)
18. My mother/father allowed me to influence them to say "yes." (H) (O) (S) (R) (N)
19. My mother/father encouraged and respected my opinions on topics. (H) (O) (S) (R) (N)
20. My mother/father knew who I truly was and understood me. (H) (O) (S) (R) (N)
21. My mother/father knew my strengths and helped me understand them. (H) (O) (S) (R) (N)
22. My mother/father helped me understand my personality and learning style. (H) (O) (S) (R) (N)
23. My mother/father taught me how to do new things. (H) (O) (S) (R) (N)
24. My mother/father showed belief in me to accomplish things. (H) (O) (S) (R) (N)
25. My mother/father encouraged me when I was failing or unsure. (H) (O) (S) (R) (N)
26. My mother/father prayed with me and taught me about God and values. (H) (O) (S) (R) (N)
27. My mother/father were comfortable talking to me about sex. (H) (O) (S) (R) (N)
28. My mother/father made me feel like I belonged in my family. (H) (O) (S) (R) (N)

About the Author

Our individual attachment style plays a crucial role in the quality of our relationships and is often the strongest predictor of how secure and connected we feel with others. Yet, many people remain unaware of their own attachment style—let alone how to shift from an unhealthy style to one that fosters safer, healthier, and more fulfilling relationships. Fortunately, awareness around attachment theory has grown significantly in the past decade. As this framework becomes increasingly central to modern mental health discussions, Marc Cameron is emerging as a leading voice in bringing this awareness.

Marc and his wife have taken up the mantle of leading the How We Love brand, the organization founded by renowned attachment experts Milan and Kay Yerkovich. Building on the foundation of their groundbreaking book *How We Love* (with over 400,000 copies sold), Marc helps readers uncover and understand the attachment style they developed in childhood. He offers clear, practical steps for moving toward a secure attachment style, providing the insight and direction so many are seeking to improve both their inner lives and relationships.